Do what you can, with what you have, where you are.
—THEODORE ROOSEVELT

INCREASE YOUR
PERSONAL
PRODUCTIVITY

YOUR GUIDE TO INTENTIONAL LIVING & DOING MORE OF WHAT YOU ENJOY

JOHN MARTIN

Published and Distributed by

SOUND WISDOM
PO Box 310
Shippensburg, PA 17257-0310

717-530-2122

info@soundwisdom.com
www.soundwisdom.com

While efforts have been made to verify information contained in this publication, neither the author nor the publisher assumes any responsibility for errors, inaccuracies, or omissions. While this publication is chock-full of useful, practical information, it is not intended to be legal or accounting advice. All readers are advised to seek competent lawyers and accountants to follow laws and regulations that may apply to specific situations. The reader of this publication assumes responsibility for the use of the information. The author and publisher assume no responsibility or liability whatsoever on the behalf of the reader of this publication.

Cover/Jacket design by Eileen Rockwell
Interior designed by Terry Clifton

ISBN 13 TP: 978-1-64095-063-4
ISBN 13 eBook: 978-1-64095-064-1

For Worldwide Distribution, Printed in the U.S.A.
2 3 4 5 6 / 23 22 21 20 19

*For Joe—who taught me
by example to just do it.*

CONTENTS

Preface 1

CHAPTER 1   Set and Systematize Your Goals 5

CHAPTER 2   Maintain the Machine 31

CHAPTER 3   Manage Distractions 55

CHAPTER 4   Value the Process 75

CHAPTER 5   Motivate Yourself 97

CHAPTER 6   Complete, Evaluate, Begin Again . . 123

PREFACE

How can you maximize your personal productivity?

By personal productivity I mean the work we do on a regular basis. Our work provides a big part of our purpose in life, so we want to be good at it. We want to produce high quality through our efforts. And, we want to achieve all that we aspire to accomplish.

If you want to increase your output, this book offers *six key initiatives* or checkpoints that can be used as a structure to follow or as a resource of tools to maximize your efforts in reaching your personal goals.

We'll start by looking at goals. One way to boost your productivity is to *create a system of goals* customized to your work, personality, and preferences. Setting goals is a major part of the process. Visualizing the end result, working hard on what you're good at while outsourcing what you're not, and tailoring your goal system so that it is both attainable and challenging is foundational to increasing your personal productivity.

In addition to having a formula for achieving goals, you'll want to make sure to take care of your body—the "machine"—and *maintain your health* to maximize your ability to work for high-quality results.

Once you are in the daily grind, *manage distractions* so you can achieve your goals consistently. Soon, you will start paying more attention to your goals and less to distractions—and work becomes something you look forward to. You *value the process* and enjoy working.

Of course, not every day will be the best day. And you will find yourself in moods of laziness or frustration that seem to last too long. We'll look at a variety of ways to *motivate yourself* during these times when you don't feel like working toward your goals.

Eventually, you will be back into the process and you reach a point where you are close to reaching a major goal. This is the place where so many fail for one reason: they don't finish their work. Or they don't let go of it. When you've invested so much of your life into something, it is hard to say it's finished. We'll look at ways to close out the deal, *finish the project*, and send out the product.

After you reach a major goal, it's time to celebrate! But not for long. After feeling the fulfillment of a completed goal, it's time to *evaluate* the process and decide how you might *adjust* it for the next one.

Then it will be time to *begin again.* A new project, a new set of goals, and a new process for doing more of what you do well.

We'll also look at ways to:

- overcome the inhibitions of the perfectionist;

- create habits and goals that enhance productivity;

- increase productivity through careful communication;

- and much more.

SET AND SYSTEMATIZE
YOUR GOALS

What is the force behind people who produce at quality or quantity much higher than others? Writers who write numerous books, salespeople who sell more volume than their peers, artists who create more art, and entrepreneurs who get more done in one day than most do in a week. What allows this?

What gives them the ability to excel in producing results, content, sales, art, or whatever their field may be? It can't be only circumstances like not having a day job or having tons of money or having some kind of special gene passed on. If this were the case, we wouldn't see people from all different walks of life becoming high-level producers. Is it talent alone? Is it some secret? Is there a universal truth that can give someone the knowledge, inspiration, and tools to produce at extraordinary levels?

I've studied my habits and others' habits and methods of work and the different approaches to workdays, processes, and the arduous actions of building something from the ground up. I've studied what makes people quit or not try at all, why we get distracted and never finish (but continually work on it), or finish but never ship the product.

I searched for the answers to my own frustrations at producing, which include: procrastination, distraction, being swayed too easily by the words and suggestions of others, starting too many projects at once, and so on. One thing I learned is that just because a method worked for one person doesn't mean it will work for another.

When you get into the details of starting and finishing project after project and achieving goal after goal, you will find that it is a highly individualized strategy that is specific to each person. Some people swear by setting aside a certain time in the day to work on their craft. Some people work at it all day. Others when the inspiration strikes them. Some swear by riding the momentum, so when they get going they don't stop until they have to. Others produce higher quality and quantities of work when they are under pressure—up against tight deadlines, rather than when they have lots of time.

Within individual fields, careers, and crafts, there will be unlimited numbers of differing strategies and tools for creating and producing more. In these pages, I explore a macro-level set of tools, guidelines, or principles by which anyone can learn to produce and finish more projects and do more work—no matter what kind of work they do.

IDENTIFY AND LINE UP WITH YOUR STRENGTHS

When you know what you are good at, and most of us do, it's not hard to focus on a certain line of work or career trajectory or line of goals. If you don't know what you are good at, make finding out your top priority and start by trying lots of different paths and occupations. There are so many options right now such as non-traditional educational opportunities that lead to diverse career possibilities including, for example, internet retail sales and starting your own home-based business through social media channels.

Don't try to fit into stereotypes or feel pressured to go a certain direction due to your upbringing or your gender, there is no need for that in today's world. Believe in your abilities and your work ethic. Try what you find interesting and keep an open mind.

Try what you find interesting and keep an open mind.

Back to knowing your strengths—if you are in a career that complements your skill set, then you already know that you are the only inhibitor of your own productivity. The sky is the limit, and you are on the right track. If you aren't in this ideal situation yet, but you know people who are, talk to them about it. Learn how they got where they are and how it feels to be living that life.

Someone is good at sales, yet working in accounting and wondering why he isn't being as productive as he wants to be. Someone is working with words when she should be working with numbers, and so on. Learn and know your strengths and put your time into growing in those strengths while accepting your weaknesses. Your weaknesses are nothing to be ashamed of, as everybody has their own.

Spend your time doing what you are meant to do. You probably know what it is and you can hear it in that still, small voice in your mind that makes you want to do the things that you are interested in. You can feel it in the way you feel after succeeding at it or being complimented in this area. Maybe you feel there are several paths that would fit this description. List a few skills that you are good at and interested in. Focus on the one that you are strongest in; but in any case, find those strengths and line up with them.

Sometimes your physical body limits you. If you are interested in playing football for a living, but you are 150 pounds as an adult, then you aren't likely to succeed with this goal. But there are many other opportunities surrounding football. You could be a sportswriter, a broadcaster, a physical therapist specializing in sports, etc.

Follow your line of strengths and interests as much as you can in order to optimize your starting point of production. From there, it will be much easier to do the work necessary to learn and grow and be the best you can be at whatever you choose.

START SOMEWHERE, BUT START

People stall when they feel the path isn't clear. They think there is something missing. They believe that there is some epiphany or moment of clarity that will shine a light on exactly what it is they should be doing— something that they are wildly passionate about that will quickly get them from where they are to where they want to be. More often than not, the only thing they are missing is *starting.*

Think about it—no doubt there's something you like to do, something you are good at, something that you know you are gifted in. It may not be super exciting or groundbreaking, you may not be the next great musician or actor, but there is work you would be content doing. Work in which you could find joy and satisfaction—if you would only try.

Start by looking at what you consume for entertainment. Or think about education—what would you want to go back to school to learn? What field or subject would you study that would land you the career you want?

The point is to start. Start out of the necessity of getting out of the unsatisfying work you are doing.

All the following principles still apply even if you have not yet found what you love. If you do the things you have to do with awareness, diligence, and with the motive of being aware enough to figure out the next step for you, the path will show itself. And then you will apply that same attitude and work ethic to that step, and so on and so on, and before you know it, you will be doing what you like at a level of productivity you could have never dreamed yourself capable.

Start today, not one day. Start before you are ready.

WHAT DO YOU WANT?

What were you interested in before you became practical?

It's important to maintain a sense of urgency about deciding this part because it can be a real hang-up for many people. Many think, ponder, ask, second-guess, and never start doing what they are interested in or good at because they are waiting for an answer so obvious that they don't see it.

You have to be realistic about your choice. If you want to do something different, something that you enjoy doing more than what you do now, then you have to choose something that you would rather do. It's not so hard.

We overcomplicate the decision by trying to identify ourselves too concretely. Or by thinking we have to be extremely skilled in our choice of field. There has to be self-awareness in our choice, but also believe in our ability to become skilled in this area. When we think back to a common denominator in our lives, we can find what we're good at and renew a love for this gift or interest. It's a reciprocal effect.

There might be twenty other ways you would rather be spending your time, that's fine. Pick one. Maybe you'll end up going down one of the other options at a later time; maybe you'll blend a couple of your interests into one endeavor. More is possible once you *start* down a path—but it has to be a path different from the one with which you are currently dissatisfied. The important thing is to start something that is interesting to you and learn the skills required to become successfully productive.

Many people don't know what they want. But they know what they *don't* want, and that is what they are trying to buy their way out of. So, you can start from this place, too. Research different fields of work. As long as you are honest about it with yourself and your motives are sincere, let your search be an outlet for your discontent rather than numbing yourself with mindless entertainment. Think of it as finding an escape route from the nightmare you find yourself in on a daily basis. Once you know what you want, you can double down on your strengths to do more and find more fulfillment as you reach your goals.

Many don't know what they want—but they know what they *don't* want!

WE WANT OPTIONS

If you aren't looking for a specific career, amount of money, or place to live, if you're not trying to retire in five years or some other specific goal, but you understand that you want to increase your level of production, you might be hard-pressed to say exactly why. It can almost always be boiled down to *options*.

We want choices. We don't want to have to do only one job our whole life; even if we end up doing that, our daily goals relate to having options. As humans, we don't like the feeling of restriction in most cases. We want to have a Plan B if Plan A doesn't work out. Or if we get bored with working at one task, it is nice to have the skills to do another.

Options. We give ourselves options when we produce at high levels consistently. Develop an exceptional work ethic, a formula for success, and you can use it in a variety of situations. Whether in sales or marketing or creative endeavors or whatever else you might have a level of competence.

It's the formula of production that will give you different options. And, of course, the money that likely follows your rate of production will give you options as well. But if you can't say exactly why you want to learn to do more of what you do well, think of the options. That's motivation enough.

FOCUS

The reason I recommend choosing only one path to start is that it makes it easier to focus. When you specialize in a field, you can learn more about it, spend more time doing it, and thus improve at both your craft and at finishing what you start. Starting too many careers or not focusing on one above another leads to burnout and feelings of failure.

The following are important aspects to consider:

- Pick a direction and go hard for it.

- Go until you are sure that either it was the wrong path or that you have taken your abilities and opportunities as far as they can go in this field, and now it is time to change directions and try something else.

- Focusing makes it easier on your mind, which is tempted to go full speed down fourteen different avenues.

- Limit this temptation as much as possible by specializing your interest and working on making everything you do tie into this area of interest.

- Focus your mind on setting up goals for this area of interest.

- Set up goals that will get you one step closer to whatever your major goal is for this field of choice.

CUSTOMIZE A SYSTEM OF GOALS

I use a system that breaks down my goals into three descriptions: 1) daily goals; 2) major goals; and 3) ultimate goal. (You can name your goals whatever you want: short-term, mid-term, and long-term goals work just as well.) The daily goals serve the major goals that serve my ultimate goal.

Daily goals aren't necessary 365 days a year, but they could be. Then the major goals would be things that are comprised of the daily goals all of which serve the ultimate goal. The ultimate goal is the one that might take years of your life (usually) to reach. It is the one that when you get there, you can feel like you are on the summit of the mountain you just climbed—and you can take time to reflect and then decide on a new ultimate goal.

For example, right now my daily goal is to write 1,000 words. My major goal is to finish this book. My ultimate goal is to earn enough income from writing to write full-time. When I finish my daily goal, it feels great to have completed it, no matter how rough the rest of the day is. When I achieve or complete my major goal, I take a short break and then begin work on my next major goal, which in my case is another book. At that point, it's time to set daily goals again, etc.

Think about how you can break down your ultimate goal into a system that works for you. You want to start with your biggest goal and figure out how to break it down at least into weekly, preferably daily segments as that's most immediate and achievable. Then create intermediate levels of achievement toward your most important goal as you see fit. Once you have the system down, you can start making it part of your program, and it eventually becomes habitual. There are many ways to do this, use your creativity to come up with one that works for you.

In addition to your career or work goals, this systematization method can be used for various other parts of your life in which you might have goals. You can create a system for achieving success in fitness or diet or even in a hobby by setting up a similar system that makes the doing almost automatic.

THE SIDE HUSTLE

If you are in the position where you need to keep working at your full-time job, but you want to start something on the side, a creative endeavor, a home-based business, etc., set up your goals and production system accordingly. With the tools and connections available through the internet, never before in history has there been as much opportunity for anyone to set up a home-based business.

Keep working hard at your day job; don't slack in favor of your side gig. Just set goals that allow for both. When you work hard, as a rule, you'll work as hard in your side hustle as in your regular job. The momentum from one will feed the other.

FOLLOW THROUGH ON YOUR GOALS

Now that you have found and begun to focus on an area of interest, the next step is to follow through on the system of goals you have created. Habitually follow through. If you are finding that you are not following through, evaluate what might be inhibiting your progress or causing you to stop and possibly making it impossible for you to finish.

First, are your goals attainable? If you are setting daily goals that you are not hitting more often than you are, take a hard look. If you are giving 100 percent and putting in enough time, yet still falling short, it may be that the goal needs to be adjusted to be achievable.

After evaluating and finding your goals are doable, then examine the effort you are giving to each. Time management—are you putting in work at available occasions for sustained periods of time? Are you still spending the same number of hours on entertainment as you were before you started this high-level production journey? If so, this is something that needs to be examined and adjusted. Sacrifices must be made.

Habits—are you still consuming poor quality food, negative entertainment and information, or neglecting to exercise? If so, make adjustments.

Don't be discouraged if you can't drop all bad habits or use every spare moment to work on your goal. This is a gradual change, and your goal is to begin to hit your daily goals and make that your main focus. The habits and time management are secondary. Work on making your bad habits less important in your life than your goals.

 # Work on making your bad habits less important than your goals.

When you start adopting this perspective, your habits will slowly change on their own as your body will want to feel a certain way in order to produce more. You will start thinking more and more about the goals you've set in a day and then you will squeeze in time to work on them whenever you can instead of procrastinating or worrying about some other obligation that used to cause you anxiety and lost time.

CONSCIOUS GOAL-SETTING

It's easy to be distracted or lost in the past or day-dreaming of the future when we have no goals. When we set, see, and serve our goals—time (past and future) is irrelevant. It stops existing as the human construct of seconds, minutes, hours, days, weeks, months, and years. Eventually this idea of looking back into the past begins to fade altogether—only to be acknowledged with intentionality.

In fact, to accomplish our goals, we have to be grounded in the present! Awareness and consciousness in the present is what allows us to achieve great feats. Accomplishments that take lifetimes to complete are completed moment by moment. Actually, we all have goals, but we're not always conscious of them or intentional about setting them.

For example, your goal might be to wake up early enough to get to your job on time, so you don't get fired. Another goal is to work hard enough while on the job so you can achieve the goal of getting paid to achieve the goal of buying lunch and dinner to make it through the day. Maybe once you get through the day, your goal is to get comfortable on the couch with another goal of finding something decent to watch on TV, for the goal of enjoying a relaxing evening.

These goals might be said to be necessary to your survival, yet they are set and served almost unconsciously.

When we consciously set goals, we achieve more.

If you want to build something that lasts, you have to be conscious and aware of the process. The process involves setting, seeing, and serving goals.

VISUALIZE GOALS

Let's talk about seeing our goals. This is an exercise of the mind. Something you're often reminded of—especially if you're a parent—is that we used to be skilled at using our mind to construct fantastic worlds. Kids are imaginative. Visualizing goals is when we need to channel our inner child's openness to possibility. As adults concerned about providing, it becomes natural to see goals as material gains or profits. But those goals are not always satisfying or motivating.

If you are not motivated by riches, figure out the feeling you are looking for by accomplishing the goal you wish to accomplish. Is it the idea of freedom? Is it the comfort of a house? Is it spiritual? Is it a state of mind or maybe an occupation? Usually, it's some combination of several of these aspirations.

To help you visualize, I suggest making vision boards. Paste pictures that represent your goals on a poster board and place it somewhere you will frequently see it. Vision boards are a form of positive conditioning and the images in your mind give you strength and motivation to sit down (or stand up) and do the work.

This beginning point of motion will start to illuminate a path forward, and eventually you will experience a strong, clear place of contentment and clarity such as you have never felt before. This path will become your primary goal, your perfect place of existence.

This path will become your perfect place of existence.

See your goals. See your idealized lifestyle. Put it in pictures and write it down. But above all, let it appear and rest in your mind until it becomes an unrelenting stimulus to action, an action that will eventually become your primary source of fulfillment. Take action and see your goal.

SET GOALS THAT ENHANCE PRODUCTIVITY

The first rule for setting goals is to set goals that you can reach; and more importantly, set goals that you *want* to reach. You want your smaller goals to be part of a bigger one. You want your daily goals to contribute toward your ultimate goal—and this is how you enhance productivity, through setting goals.

As you reach these goals on a daily basis, you will be impressed. These are goals you likely have never reached before, and you will be surprised that you do. This surprise will turn to motivation as you realize that if it is possible now to get done what you have, then it is possible to do more. Then you can set a slightly higher goal and a slightly shorter timeline, both of which lead you closer to your ultimate goal.

We have to have targets if we want to hit them. One way to make this idea of setting goals and chasing goals more palatable is to make the target big and general enough that it can be hit. Make it something that you want, something that you know you can achieve if you would only stay with it long enough to finish it—like that 1,000-piece puzzle. You have to sit down at the table with it to start.

You want to put yourself in a frame of mind that will give you the opportunity to succeed—provided you do the work. But if you're in a spot where you're intimidated or overwhelmed, you might not begin. You might not sit down at the table covered in puzzle pieces or at the desk with the blank page. So make your goal desirable and attainable.

SETTING DAILY GOALS

This means setting reasonable amounts of work to be done in reasonable amounts of time. Now obviously, *reasonable* is subjective, let me explain. Set goals that are broken apart from your overriding goal for a project to be completed. For example, if you are trying to make ten new sales *each month,* maybe your goal is to establish a certain number of contacts or leads *per day.*

Start by thinking of a time when you were successful with a goal like the one you have now. We've already established that the overriding goal is attainable; you know in your heart that you have the competence to achieve it. So now think back to the time when you did something similar and break it down so you can see on the micro level, on the daily level what you are capable of accomplishing.

When you set daily goals that you know you can achieve and when you look at them from afar, you can see how achieving those daily goals will allow you to complete the overall project by a certain time, you have a roadmap. This is your plan.

Stick to it daily and you will get the boost of energy and confidence that comes with achieving your self-established goals day after day. And as you get closer to your main goal as a result, you will feel more motivated to do more. So on some days, you will start doing more than your established goal just because you're in the zone, and you want to keep working.

On the other hand, do not be discouraged for long if you miss your daily goal. Tomorrow is a new day and you will make up for it tomorrow. Always make up what you missed plus that day's goal of production. This way, you will remember the feelings of having to do two days' work in one, and it will motivate you to avoid this when possible.

EXPERIENCE VERSUS INTELLIGENCE

So many ideas are intellectually understood (known) without being experienced. When it comes to producing at high levels, you don't realize what is possible until you experience it—until you hit goals that you've never hit before even though you might have had them in mind for years. It's intellectually explained, sure, your confidence increases with your output or your breakthrough of self-imposed limits, but it really can't be understood from a second-person point of view unless you've been through it.

Maybe it's the old "chicken or the egg" discussion, but I see the experience as the cornerstone of the belief that motivates the doing. When you see people converting crazy amounts of sales, or nailing the marketing of products on a consistent, repeated basis, it's not because they have some secret hack or that they have a more motivated, ambitious spirit, it's because they have the experience.

The way you get that experience is setting goals and pushing the boundaries of your goal-setting habits, coming up with a plan and hitting that goal. Then doing it again. Eventually, you will get to a point where you look at what you just achieved, and say, "I remember when I didn't believe I could do this."

This might be a goal that intellectually you *knew* you could accomplish, but for years you didn't. Why? A lack of experience. Get those reps in. I've heard the example used about push-ups. The only way you can get better at doing push-ups is not by reading about it, not by listening to a seminar about it or watching videos about it. It's by *doing* push-ups. One day you can do five and then ten, and so on. Simple, but needs to be experienced to be understood.

FOCUS ON YOUR CRAFT

So not only are you doing more of what you like, you want to focus on getting better at what you like as well. Doing more will help in this arena, but also learning from people who are super productive at what you want to be doing. I think this might come secondary to actually doing, but especially if you are young, take time to learn from the people who have lived the kind of life you would like to live.

Focusing on mentorship or learning from others' experiences as well as getting better or stronger at your craft will help boost your productivity in three ways:

1. When you practice your craft, eventually you are going to make or create or do something that is valuable and worthwhile, so even in practice, in that rough draft, in that practice sales pitch, in that first video cut, you are producing, you are making something.

2. By looking at others and learning from others' experiences, you may get creative ideas on avenues you can take or products you can build and put together to provide value. You may not have thought of them if you didn't read that author's book, go to her seminar, or visit his social media page.

3. Learning from the people you admire— learning the pitfalls and wrong turns and missteps that they made will save you time that would've been wasted and can now be used in productive ways.

In summation, doing more of what you are good at and put on earth to do while learning how to do it better is the starting point. Looking for and learning from others who have been on the road you are now on and have succeeded in getting where you want to go will be extremely useful to you in achieving your goals and learning about the life you are living.

Let's look at some ways to prepare for this journey of visualizing, setting, and following through on your goals to increase and maximize your personal productivity.

CHAPTER 2

MAINTAIN THE MACHINE

S tart treating your body as a machine. You may think of being a machine as something negative, perhaps robotic or just mechanical. But if you think about being more productive, machines are definitely productive—unless they are worn-out or broken. Furthermore, if you experience living life like a machine, it's not so bad as you might imagine—such as there are fewer surprises as you accept everything and are more aware. I know awareness doesn't seem to fit with machine-like, but it does. You see, we are self-aware machines that can accomplish unbelievable amounts of achievements, feats, and productions...if we first believe it.

So believe it about yourself, turn yourself into the highly effective, high-energy, high-quantity producing machine that you are. Start by thinking about your body, what you put into it, and what you want to make with it.

What do you want to be? What do you want to do or to experience in life? Who do you wish to become? The answers to these questions will be the foundation for your machine. No matter what it is that you want to do, it becomes easier when you do it through a machine. So build your body as a machine designed to produce at massive levels and quantities.

This is the beginning of your productive part of life. Today, right now, start doing. Start building, start making, and start shipping it out to the world. People are waiting for your work. When you discover this machine, this ability within you to produce at levels you previously thought impossible, you will face other challenges. There will be new goals to achieve, mountains to climb, and rivers to cross.

FITNESS

Truth is, I don't like this part either, but you have to get your fitness game right in order produce at high levels. Keep your health in check so you can feel good for longer. Start by walking. Take a walk every day. It is useful to incorporate another form of exercise too such as lifting weights two to three times per week. Or swimming, bicycling, yoga, or a sport you like.

Just a few of the benefits of taking a daily walk: increased heart strength and better management of hypertension, high cholesterol, stress, etc. Walking reduces your risk for heart disease and improves bone strength and balance. Exercise helps your productivity as it allows time for you to process thoughts and work through things mentally while your body is working physically, allowing for great connection of thoughts and ideas.

Sometimes exercise also works as an "unload" function. We can take a break from the intellectual stimuli and the information "overload" of the day and simply let our bodies work out. Lifting weights or running or walking can be perfect forms of meditation and emptying of the mind.

DIET

I'm not a dietician, but one tip that has always helped me get started on a better diet or a more healthier way of living is to eat breakfast and limit caffeine intake by drinking more water throughout the day. Another way is to plan your meals.

You can prepare your meals for two or three days ahead in containers, which eliminates a lot of time spent thinking about what to eat or where to eat, how much to spend, etc. Prep your food and eat at regularly scheduled times whenever possible. Eat before you are hungry.

Cut up celery sticks, peppers, broccoli, and add baby carrots to the mix. Pack some grapes and sliced apples. Eating fresh vegetables and fruits throughout the day helps you to avoid binge eating at night or at meal times. When you eat too much, you feel lethargic and you are less likely to put in extra time on your goals.

Try to maintain the balance between when and what you eat and not only will you be surprised at how much energy you feel, you will be surprised at how much you get done by not thinking about food as frequently throughout the day.

You still think about eating, but it becomes mechanical and your body knows what to do and it does it. Day in and day out. There is valuable information available about diets and what might best suit your needs, but whatever your choice of diet, look to systematize your eating habits to maximize your time and overall health.

Eat out with friends and family sometimes, but if you want to crank up your output, systematize your meals and drink more water.

SET YOUR ENVIRONMENT

Whether you work from home or somewhere else, to the best of your ability, optimize your workspace to include the aspects and items that help you be more productive. If that is a certain type of music, an audio book, quotes on the wall, a favorite desk chair or room in your house.

When I write, I like to turn on some upbeat music without lyrics. There are many videos on YouTube that feature eight solid hours of music, which you may find inspirational and keep you motivated. Wherever and whatever it is that gets you going and gives you motivation and comfort as you work, make sure you set that up for yourself each day.

If you are stuck working in a daily grind that you don't like, and there is little about the environment that you can alter or find comfort in, set your mind up for success. Some days will be rough, so you have to figure out how to do more of what you love to get you out of your current tough situation.

There is a way out. It's doing something you are good at and doing enough of it that you are able to start seeing the escape route. Get in the groove. Find a rhythm for good days of production. This goes for your daily grind and side hustle. Find that groove and stay in it as long as you can.

What are some tips for finding the groove?

- When you don't feel like working, don't. Take a break, if possible.

- When you get antsy and feel claustrophobic from being in your workspace, go. Get outside and take a walk or get in your vehicle and take a ride. That's the beautiful thing about most of our work life these days; we're not forced to be in our chairs or at our work stations for 16 hours a day.

- Go outside and get some fresh air on your lunch break.

- If you can take a ride, do so, sometimes a change of scenery can bring fresh perspective on the afternoon.

- If your job doesn't allow for outside escapes, having a cup of water and a brief, friendly chat with a friend or coworker can renew a zeal for work.

Many times, just getting outside for a bit can bring new energy to your work. Then when you get back into the day and its tedious needs and false emergencies, you can stay with it until the end. Then you are re-motivated and can put in a good day's work until it's time to shut down, or move on to your side hustle.

If you can't do that, you may need to ask some tough questions of yourself.

GO WITH RATHER THAN AGAINST YOUR NATURE

If you are generally more productive in the morning, do more in the morning. If you are disciplined and plan your time and schedule tightly in accordance with your disciplined ways, be sure to do this when you are working on your creative efforts or your side hustle. Schedule your time and stick to it if that is your modus operandi.

If you are more spontaneous and less organized, be prepared to be productive when the urge hits you and do more of it. Don't fight and try to improve your weaknesses, go heavier on your strengths.

Some work best from home, others do better by going into an office or library or cafe, somewhere away from home. Some people like to mix it up and find new places to work if all they need is an internet connection and a phone. If you have these kinds of choices, choose the environment that motivates your best work.

The best practice is in line with your nature.

We are taught and sold many times on the idea of regimented schedules of production and step-by-step procedures to increase productivity, and even systems that promise to increase creativity or results through a carefully followed set of instructions. Many of these systems or programs are based on the idea of improving your weaknesses. They attack your pain points. So if you happen to be someone who would rather sleep until noon and stay up until 3 a.m., then the sales effort will be made to help you get up early and produce in the morning like most people.

Everyone is different. The best practice is that which is in line with your nature. Some people have produced massive amounts of quality product and do high-quality work throughout the night, while many others do their best work and produce the highest quantities in the morning. Still others like to work right in the middle of the day—in the afternoon. Sometimes you have no choice. It doesn't matter when, it only matters that you do the work. Pay attention to who you are and the circumstances under which you are most likely to flourish.

DROP SELF-JUDGMENT

We are too hard on ourselves. We are too negative toward our own progress or lack thereof.

If you are someone who has notebooks full of ideas and rarely follow any of them out to a productive level, it's okay. You don't need to judge yourself and consider it a waste of time, maybe your strength is coming up with ideas. Maybe you could sell your ideas. Maybe you simply enjoy the thought process behind coming up with ideas and concepts. Know that it is okay. Maybe you've started fifty projects and haven't completed one of them yet. Okay, well, that's better than not starting anything, right?

Beyond this, every person lives in their own time zone. We do things when it is right for us to do them.

Dropping self-judgment is a useful step in freeing up your mind to follow through with the ideas that you wish to bring to fruition. On the other hand, many of us are setting goals to do things we don't really want to do. It might be that we like the idea of being that person or accomplishing that goal, but we have no desire to do the work that is necessary. No amount of forced discipline will change that for us. We have to be in alignment with our true inclinations, strengths, and aspirations.

Like chasing money, if you're doing it for the ends, it won't bring fulfillment and will limit your productivity level.

Make the best of surprise schedule changes.

Life is full of unexpected detours in our planned journey of a day's time. Meetings have to be rescheduled, a three-hour flight turns into a ten-hour airport extravaganza, and traffic jams turn a half-hour drive into a two-hour drive, and so on. Be prepared for delays and downtime. You can take advantage of this time by having the tools with you to produce and get things done with only a little inconvenience.

Sometimes these mishaps are good for focusing our attention on an issue that needed attention but would've been shortchanged if all had gone as planned. Plenty of work can be done with a smartphone. Added to that, I recommend carrying a notebook and pen and you can be ready for any setback. Gain ground when you lose ground, and you'll never feel as though your time is wasted.

IDENTIFY INHIBITORS

What are the habits that block, slow, or halt your creativity and production? What stalls our machines? We all have habits, inclinations, or thought processes that inhibit us from creating and working as long and hard as we want. Naming those obstacles is essential to begin developing workarounds or ways to eliminate them from our lives.

Start by thinking of what most commonly derails you from working on a project that you want to finish but have not yet. Any work of passion or love that you can think of that is unfinished, why is it? What is getting in the way of completing your work?

Think of what usually happens when you are working on something but you stop before it's completed. Is it fatigue? Is it drinking or watching sports? Surfing the internet? If a computer project that you're working on, what websites do you habitually visit when you are stalling?

Whatever sidetracks you, write it down and take steps to work around it. Once you have identified and named these habits as culprits of slowing you down from reaching your goals, you will start thinking of them in a different light. Even if it is just slightly more than when you used to favor them without thinking and abandon your work, now maybe just for a couple seconds you second-guess yourself and decide not to grab that beer or start that YouTube video—and you get back to your work.

This isn't a book about overcoming bad habits, but there is plenty of available useful information on this topic that, if you apply it, will help you cut out bad habits from your life. For the purpose of this book, we are acknowledging them and bringing them to the forefront as inhibitors to your creativity and production. That alone is a step in the right direction and for some, it may be all you need to work around, through, and despite your bad habits. And maybe through this step, you will be able to replace them with more productive activities.

That is the goal at the end of the day—to be able to make a new habit out of work. Work becomes a habit of production, of creating. You care less about anything else and more about doing more work. This is the goal and it is absolutely attainable.

LET GO

A crucial part of our machine is the mind. We have to prepare mentally for stress, setbacks, frustrations, and times of annoyance. There are many ways to approach this. Some will say that fighting through those times is the only way to overcome them. I see *not trying so hard* as a better way to work around the mental roadblocks that inevitably arise in our efforts.

Our inherent and culturally reinforced drive for security causes an inner tension that inhibits creativity and productivity. We chase an illusory security through more money, more possessions, more accomplishments, more, more, more. What if we let go?

Take a deep breath, exhale slowly, and be present.

What if we could let go of our self-importance? What if we could grasp that we are not the bodies we see in the mirror, or our names, or the stories we tell ourselves about who we are? What if we understood that we were life itself and that we were already perfect? Suddenly, our actions would feel more like play than work. Stress, pressure to improve or to gain, these ideas and motivations are counter to the mindset (or lack thereof) needed to be open to fresh ideas and inspiration.

What are you stressed out about? Take a deep breath, exhale slowly and be present. This moment is what you have, that's it. This moment of life is what you are, not your past, or your position at your job, or even your name. You exist only in this moment and if you work at experiencing this moment rather than holding on to your identity, you will find great freedom to be whatever you wish. You must let go of the desire for security and control and realize it is only further dividing you from the reality of the present.

Open yourself to this truth and watch your productivity increase. Watch your cares become secondary and your passion gather and rise to prominence as you become obsessed with doing the work that you choose rather than focusing most of your energy on that which you do not.

Maybe you say you can't do this. Maybe you have children and a mortgage and other responsibilities. Maybe your job requires hard physical labor and not only do you not have time to work at something else while on the job, you also are physically exhausted at the end of the day. To this I say, start small but start somewhere. I wrote my first e-book while on lunch breaks at work. Any chance you get, work on what you want.

By letting go, by not trying as hard, what you do is you let go of the weight of self-importance. This is contradictory, paradoxical thinking at its finest. While you are trying to produce more and get more done so you can perhaps quit your day job or earn more money—at the same time—let go of that as a driving force. Let go of the idea of *need* and be present in the moment of creation or work.

If this concept sounds weird to you, then you should try it and your skepticism will lead to less trying and desire. When you focus on your wants and your goals and what you are trying to achieve with your actions or behavior, you consequently fill your mind with thoughts that block other thoughts and ideas from rising into that space.

DELIBERATION

Understanding that we will naturally want to do more of what gives us pleasure, another tactic is to find pleasure in what we are already doing. Prentice Mulford, in his book *Thoughts are Things*, writes, "Pleasure is the sure result of placing thought or force on the thing we are doing now." No matter what your occupation, build the habit of intensely focusing on the task at hand down to the smallest detail.

As you do this, it becomes enjoyable and you begin looking forward to it. Consequently, the quality of your work improves. With your newfound, intense interest in the process comes the desire to do it more often—and that is the secret. Influence yourself. Be patient with the process.

Being deliberate is not about being slow; it's about being intentionally focused on the action taking place at your fingertips. What are you doing right now? Pay attention to every aspect of it that you can think of. This habit of deliberating on what you are doing will be inspirational in producing more and of higher quality.

Each thought you have and capture gives place to another thought and another. If you can keep those thoughts pushing toward and swirling around one topic, now you've found a source of ideas that can't be beat. The starting point was paying attention to what you were doing.

So especially while you are working on your side hustle, your dream life, pay careful attention to each step of it from a mental and physical perspective. See the aesthetics and the wonder of it. Really accept and internalize the miracle that is life at work creating and making and forming and shaping and living the dream. All of this is mental preparation and practice for establishing a personal production process that works for you.

TAKE A BREAK

It's important to take a break every once in a while. You don't want to burn yourself out and cost yourself valuable production time later. For this reason and reasons of health, relationships, and quality work, schedule time off when you need it. You'll know it when your body starts telling you with fatigue or illness or other symptoms. Maybe your family relationships or your friendships or business relationships start showing some signs of strain and stress; these are your indicators to stop and reset.

Many times the best ideas come to you when you've been away from your craft and your production for a while. Try getting away from it, living outside of it, letting your mind empty itself of thoughts related to your work. This can be just the thing needed when in a creative slump or a work-related funk.

KEEP YOUR WORK AREA ORGANIZED

I had a hard time with this one as I used to consider myself one of those messy genius types. As it turns out, I'm not a genius, but my work area is a mess. Some days we are too caught up in working to take time to organize and get rid of things we no longer need, but this is a helpful task to undertake in order to be more productive.

Take some time to clean up your workspace. It may mean re-shelving books, organizing paperwork into manageable piles, making a list and throwing out old ones (consolidating your lists), cleaning your work area of sandwich crumbs, spilled drinks—you get the idea.

Try to make being organized part of your routine to improve your thinking and getting more done. It's amazing how much those few minutes of rummaging around looking for something can add up to. Not only that, but being organized can make your thinking less cluttered as well.

EXERCISE TO CONCENTRATE

It can be a challenge to stay focused and get work done while sitting at a desk or working at a computer. If you are someone who is more inclined to be physically active, and you typically work physical jobs or whatever, it makes it even more difficult to do graphic design type work, or computer work, writing, etc.

When you find yourself unable to concentrate and unwilling to sit down in front of a computer, take a few deep breaths and then give yourself five minutes. If possible, take a brisk walk around the parking lot, do push-ups, or some other physical exercise to give release to the excess energy built up within you. While you're walking and breathing deeply, you can voice-record task lists or ideas into your phone.

When you return to your desk and sit down, allow your breathing to resume its regular pace and select the next (or first) item on your list to begin working on.

Another option is to use a standing desk. There are many variations that allow for the same work you do sitting at your desk to be done while standing.

MENTAL FOCUS VERSUS TIME MANAGEMENT

There is a ton of focus placed on time management, and certainly this is important; but I think if you can learn to habitually manage your mind, time management will improve. When you tell yourself you *need* to get things done, you often struggle and fight distraction, interruption, and procrastination following this train of thought.

When you tell yourself, I *need* to concentrate, etc., you put restrictions on your mind. Your mind battles them with every thought and distraction imaginable and puts this interruptive, disjointed energy into the universe, which reacts with visits from colleagues, phone calls, unexpected problems.

Instead, place your mental focus on your strengths, on the enjoyable aspects of what you "need" to get done, knowing full well that you will get those things done in time. Focus on the activities that motivate you to work harder and longer and more. Focus on doing more of the things you want to do.

MINDFULNESS

Resting your mind is becoming a necessity in today's fast-paced world. Basically, meditation is about emptying your mind. When you are able to shut down the thought process—the constant flow of ideas, worries, memories, predictions—you can make room for new ideas and creativity and inspiration to arise. It's a way of renewing the mind.

Mindfulness takes practice, but even starting with just a few minutes in the morning, will help. Find a place to be alone and where it is quiet (as much as possible) and try to sit still and feel the physical sensations without naming them, letting the thoughts go without examining them, eventually letting your mind become completely still.

Like anything new, it will take many attempts to become proficient at this, but the more you are able to achieve stillness of mind, the more peaceful your world will become. You will be more productive when you begin to work from a place of strength and inspiration instead of a place of stress and need. You will be mentally interrupted less frequently.

And you will also find that you don't need to sit in the lotus position alone in a room perfectly quiet. With practice, you will be able to achieve this state of non-striving awareness in the mind under many different circumstances.

Sometimes the solution to a long-time problem can come following meditation as the process allows for fresh thoughts and perspectives to replace the ones that had been spinning endlessly within your mind.

The mind is the key to unlocking greater productivity. In the next chapter, we look at more ways to focus the mind.

CHAPTER 3

MANAGE DISTRACTIONS

How can you enter into a productive state of mind?

Being in a productive state of mind enables us to maintain a sustained focus to produce outlandish amounts of work. I use the work of writing as examples because that's what I do, but these principles of production will work for every industry or field. How do we intentionally enter a state of mind that allows us to work consistently without significant stoppage for extended periods of time? Does it first happen by accident and then we replicate it?

What is the secret to controlling your mind for this purpose?

First things first, limit your distractions. Depending on what you're doing, turn off your phone and computer, if possible. The internet, email, texting—these are incredibly distracting staples of our modern, everyday lives. Most of us simply do not live without them. They are ingrained in our day-to-day existence; and in fact, our brains are adapting to the rewards and increased usage of mobile technology. Observe people in their vehicles or walking around looking down at their smart phones. It's no longer simply fodder for art or comedy, it's society. Our usage is instinctual.

Because of this, we are less likely to notice the amount of time spent using our phones. We don't notice them as distracting forces to our production. It's almost as if grabbing our phone to check our social media, the news, weather, texts, or emails have become the equivalent of getting up to get a drink or use the bathroom. But it's not; it's not the same as satisfying a necessary physical need.

So don't grab that phone or check your email. Keep working! One way to help in this area is to turn off the audible alerts on your phone. We are conditioned to respond and at least look at the text or the call when an alert prompts us. Break this habit and you will find yourself getting more done for longer periods of time.

Eliminate distracting habits.

Can you do without a phone while you work? If your phone is what you use to do your work, that's different. When you're using it, it's not using you. I understand that people do work from their phone and also much of our daily communication happens from this device. But for many of us, it is a significant distraction and even an obstacle to what we might accomplish.

I'll often write in notebooks as a way of eliminating the habits of checking email or other websites that are part of working daily on a computer. Then I type my words up later. Yes, it adds a bit of time, but I have found that it actually saves me time. It allows me to maintain the creativity and inspiration that comes from working uninterrupted for extended stretches.

Sometimes interruptions are unavoidable. But you can still return to your work and resume that momentum and creativity. As long as you come back, pick up your tools, and get to work, the inspiration will follow. So you limit distractions to the most basic needs of what you are doing.

What else?

MULTITASKING AND THE POWER OF ASSOCIATION

Sometimes parts of your production process can be detrimental and distracting. If you're doing two things at once—both producing results toward your goal—and you are good at this, no problem. Keep it up. If you start seeing quality issues or your efficiency starts to suffer in the process, it's worth taking a look at separating those parts of your process and doing one thing at a time.

Notice when you get distracted and turn that distraction into production by using the distraction as a trigger mechanism to get back to work. When you are pacing around, lost in your thoughts, avoiding the work you don't want to do, use that as a sign to get to work.

It might sound odd, but the power of association within the mind is incredible and it's worth trying.

And you can use this technique with so many different types of distraction. If it's email, associate email with some other action word that brings you back to the task at hand. The task that will help you accomplish your goals. The power of association allows you to use distractions to your advantage, and it is an unbelievable advantage to someone who understands this part of your psychological makeup.

EXPECT INTERRUPTIONS AND TEMPTATIONS TO BE DISTRACTED

When you are ready to get into your work, understand that there will be interruptions. If you are ready for them, you will not be blindsided and you won't be as susceptible to their power. Work through them, don't fall victim to their temptation. You know you can deal with them, you have in the past. So expect them and then work with and not against them. Distractions are meant to be overcome, and the more skilled you become at either avoiding distractions or eliminating distractions or working around and despite distractions, the closer you get to being the kind of production specialist, mass-volume producer, quality-creating person of your dreams.

Many people quit at the beginning of an effort to produce due to distractions that they allow to sabotage their work before they are able to establish a rhythm and get into the groove. The more this happens, the less appealing it becomes to come back and work. Days and weeks go by without any work or time spent on the project all because we are succumbing to those early interrupters. Your mind is simply not focused that early on in the process to get you the kind of concentration and drive to continue that you need.

MEETINGS

Try, in whatever circumstances this is possible, to limit your meetings to thirty minutes or less. Sometimes it may be necessary to go longer or even to schedule them for longer sections of time, but many times meetings are disorganized and can be better organized for efficiency. If you are able to start with a tighter timeline to limit the excess, do so.

When you do have meetings, have an agenda. Perhaps the meeting is to come to agreement on a decision that needs to be made. Have a goal of what you would like to accomplish by meeting with the parties involved, spell out that goal at the beginning of the meeting, and by the end of the meeting you should be able to confirm that you have reached that goal or decision. At least conclude the meeting with concrete action steps to be completed by a certain time or date.

If you are not the one in charge of meetings, as a participant you can do your part to limit the time spent by being prepared with whatever input you are asked to contribute. Anticipate questions and have the answers. Bring relevant paperwork, statistics, anything relates to the topic of the meeting, so you are ready and able to offer suggestions, solutions, or whatever necessary to move the process ahead.

DECISIONS

The often-repeated 5 x 5 rule is that if something is not going to have an impact on your life in five years, don't spend more than five minutes thinking about it. Also, there is the idea that your mind takes generally around five seconds to decide to take one action or another. The point of these two ideas is that our mind decides quickly what to do, and if we are going to be the one controlling our mind, we have to learn to make decisions, and sometimes quickly.

We make decisions we later call good and some we call bad, but our entire life is made up of these decisions. When we want to increase productivity, we're looking to buy time. If we procrastinate making decisions or we overthink them, it costs us time. But we also want to make good decisions, as a good decision might buy more time, whereas a bad one could cause us to spend more time.

If counsel or a meeting is needed, set a definite outcome that you wish to achieve and then revisit whether or not you have made the decision needed at the conclusion of your meeting.

Have faith in your decisions. Keep making them to your best judgment and roll on. The road to your goal gets longer and longer with indecision. Decide to produce, not ponder.

BE CAREFUL ABOUT CONSULTING

Go with your gut. Sometimes we seek out advice and it's helpful in making a decision, but at other times, we seek out too many sources of information, and it delays us from finishing or from making a decision.

You know who you are better than anyone else. That means you know what you want more than anyone else, and you know what you are trying to make or build more than anyone else. Trust yourself.

It is hard enough to outthink yourself—getting through the self-doubt, second-guessing, etc. that you deal with when you are trying to do something like work on building a path to your ultimate goal. Sometimes introducing too much "research" to the equation and can distract you. Your research and others' advice can pull you in a thousand different directions.

Eventually, you have to come back to the work and just simply put in the time whether that is at the keyboard writing pages, on the phone networking, or outside building a house. The answers will be clear from the action you take. Researching might give you inspiration, but working and relying on your own mind to continue the work will give you the results.

SOMETIMES, SAY NO

Not every good opportunity is good for you. Think about your goals, your long-term goals, your legacy-type goals, and consider each opportunity or proposal or idea in light of them. This will help keep you honest. There are numerous opportunities out there for those willing to put in even a little bit of extra work; and since you are going to be someone who produces constantly, more and more opportunities will come to you.

In fact, this is why we started this journey of learning how to boost our production in the first place. We like options. As you become more successful with doing more of what you love, you will be faced with that proverbial good problem of having more opportunities than time. If you don't carefully evaluate each against your own goals, you may end up losing time and other options instead. Focus on your long-term goals, not money or shiny-object options.

When people request phone calls and meetings or want to just shoot the breeze with you, be selective about accepting those requests or engaging in the water-cooler conversations. It's good to be friendly, but during crunch time, be mindful of your time. Pay attention to your interactions with others as much as your solitary actions. Be in a production mindset as much of the time as possible.

LIMIT YOUR CHOICES

We can increase our productivity by limiting our choices. This includes food, clothing, emails, apps, browser windows, anything that can cut into or distract from production time or your ability to concentrate.

Picking out your outfit for the day can become a costly distraction. The same can be true of deciding what to eat, what to purchase at the grocery store, and what to cook for your meals. It is important to eat healthy foods, but not as important to eat a different meal every day and enjoy every meal that you eat. The more you can plan and prepare ahead of time—in the evenings or whenever you might have time—the more time you can put toward your goal and the process.

For example, simplify your fashion choices. Minimize your wardrobe so you don't waste time choosing clothing and matching colors and making sure you look just right. There is value in the idea of dressing for success, but that doesn't necessarily mean suits and ties and different outfits each day.

You need to dress appropriately, but comfortably. It's fine to wear a similar outfit every day (assuming it's clean, of course). Few people notice what you wear. All of this depends on your individual situation, so tailor your clothing to fit your needs and workplace expectations. Obviously, if you work in a warehouse, you will wear basically the same outfit every day, but if you work in an office environment, you can minimize wasted time due to having too many choices by having a wardrobe that is easily mixed and matched.

Wear clean, comfortable clothing and in most situations, you'll be dressed to be productive. Too many people worry more about appearance than productivity. Give away unwanted or unused clothing and clean out the closet. Knowing you have appropriate clothes that are easy to care for will help you feel better and desire to get more done.

Narrow your choices wherever possible.

DON'T WASTE TIME

It's the easiest thing in the world to waste time. We have meetings, we procrastinate, we pace around stalling or overanalyzing decisions we need to make. You want to be on the offense if you want to do more. So do things with the mindset of attacking your goals and setting new ones.

I want to emphasize that what is considered wasting time is personal. You know when you are "killing" time or when you are enjoying yourself or working hard. The idea is to get to the point of enjoying yourself *when* you are working hard. Just be conscious of your mindset. If you are feeling badly about what you are doing, then evaluate whether that guilt is warranted or not, and act accordingly.

For me, wasting time includes surfing YouTube and watching videos, scrolling through social media posts, reading parts of one book then another, etc.

For others, wasting time may include staring at the variety of choices at the supermarket or the coffee shop or even birthday cards. We know we should just pick a product and go about our business but too many times we don't realize how much time is passing while trying to make a decision. If this is you, give yourself a specific amount of time for grocery shopping, standing in the coffee shop, etc. You could be working on your side hustle!

Each moment is your life.

POWER OF PRIORITIZATION

If you are in the daily grind with your full-time career as well as working on a side hustle, you have to set your priorities. One of them is going to be your own daily goal, but in your day job, set one or two tasks that you absolutely must get done in order to keep performing at an optimal level in your position.

Try not to set too many priority tasks or you will get overwhelmed and potentially fail to get them done each day. There will be some days when you don't get your priority tasks done, but you want to limit those days. When you cross those priority items off your list as complete, you can feel good about the rest of your day even if it wasn't as productive as you hoped—provided, of course, that you achieved your daily goal.

Setting priorities is a mental trick. When you do this repeatedly, it becomes natural to complete those priority tasks above all else. It helps focus your mind, which is a skill that you want to develop as you look to increase your personal productivity.

KNOW YOUR ENEMIES

In the daily grind, what keeps you from having a productive day? Is it some type of task that overwhelms you? Is there something that must be done that you dread doing?

For example, maybe you get overwhelmed by making phone calls. If so, make those calls first thing in the morning so that you don't have them hanging over you all day. The same goes for email. If you get stressed out by a full inbox with lots of unread, unanswered emails, then take the time to address them early so you can get other work done with a clear mind.

Is it a messy desk? Paperwork? Whatever it is that clouds your mind and distracts you from getting done what you would like to get done, is the enemy preventing you becoming the most productive version of yourself. Know them well and do whatever it takes to eliminate them from your daily grind.

CAREFUL COMMUNICATION

We can save a lot of time by listening carefully to people and reading emails with attention to the details and style of their communication. Some people prefer short and to-the-point emails while others write lengthy ones full of niceties and extraneous information. Some will do bulleted lists and still others prefer using boldface, highlighting, and capitalization to make their points clear.

These are small, but important variables to notice when communicating. Email is a massively used medium for communication, but like any form of communication, it has its flaws. It's easy to misinterpret emails if they are worded a certain way. It's also easy for some people to be aggressive, accusatory, or inflammatory with their language through an email as they are not face to face with a person. When you are talking with someone in person, there are obvious indicators of emotion and intent during communication. When reading email, you have only the sender's words and your own emotions.

Therefore, put emotions aside. Take emails lightly and never respond in kind to someone who is being rude through email. Calmly ask for respectful communication (via phone or in person if possible); and if they are unwilling to do this, then you cease communication and find another way or another contact to get done what you need to get done.

How does all this relate to increasing production? Simple. The fewer emails and phone calls that are necessary to communicate what needs to be communicated means more time for you to do your work. The less time spent being upset or offended and talking to your partner or friend about it, means more time to work toward your goal. Don't allow emotions to dictate productivity.

EMAILS AND PHONE CALLS

If you can, close your email inbox until your current work is done. Take steps to prioritize and organize your inbox. Most email providers include many tools for organizing and prioritizing your emails. It is worth taking a few minutes to learn how to use them and then make your inbox fresh and more user-friendly.

Email is a big consumer of time. It's extremely convenient, but can be a big timewaster if it is not properly controlled. Limit the amount of emails you send in a certain time period. For example, don't send more than one email every two minutes. This also will help to ensure you have taken the time to read your email and make sure it communicates clearly what you want. Read incoming emails carefully when received, and then prioritize which ones to respond to and when.

Don't answer phone calls by instinct or unnecessarily. Work on not answering the phone as a rule. Phones have "caller ID," and if you don't recognize the number or need to take the call, don't answer. The key is to control your time as much as possible; so when someone emails or texts you asking for a phone call, give them specific times when you are available.

LOOK AT THE TIME!

Time might be one of the biggest distractions of all. How often do we make decisions based on time? How much time do we have? How long will it take to do this? How many days, weeks, months, or years until we see results?

This is especially useful if you are an analytical person or someone who relies on or enjoys numbers and statistics. We are often obsessed with the idea of time and being busy and working many hours and running errands—and being a business person, parent, or student, all of these labels are closely associated with a lack of time or with the consumption of time.

It's common to hear ourselves remark or complain that we don't have enough time. To prove or disprove this remark, write down what you do in a typical 24-hour day. Take yesterday for example, or today. What did you do? Describe, write down your activities on an hourly basis.

You could even take this experiment to a weekly level. You have 168 hours in a week. If you sleep 56 of them (8 per night), you still have 112 hours. If you work 50 hours a week at your day job, you have 62 hours left. That's 62 hours in a week! Even if you go to school or work a second job or coach a kids' sports team on top of that, when you lay out the time on paper and look at it, wow! There may be a lot more time in your life than you think.

If you spend half that time on your home-based business, it would still be thirty hours a week! What could you get done in thirty hours? What about in 120 hours (one month)?

Now have a long look at the time you have and how you spend it. How many hours are spent watching TV? How many on social media? How many do you spend walking around shopping centers or malls? Playing video games?

How about the time it takes you to drive to and from work? Could you be listening to an audio book or webinar focusing on your side hustle rather than the same old music download? And if you take exercising seriously, use that time to listen to the latest news about your favorite subject.

Look again—are you sure you don't have enough time to do what you want to do?

TIME TO WORK

Now that we've covered setting goals, preparing mind, body, and workspace to reduce distractions, it's time to dig into the work. Let's look at how we can condition ourselves to look forward to the process involved in achieving more of our personal and professional goals.

CHAPTER 4

VALUE THE PROCESS

I t's the production *process* that gets you to your goal and is the life of the goal. It's the work. Once the doing becomes the goal itself, you have found the philosopher's stone. You've discovered the *real secret*— putting more value on the process than on the result.

Many times people will comment on the discipline of an achiever—someone who produces results with outstanding efficiency and volume. Highly productive people are admired or noted for their discipline. I've

noticed some who could fall into this category of productivity champions are not necessarily disciplined in
the classic sense of the term. In fact, some might be
called slovenly or undisciplined. But still, they produce.
Why? How? Because they do what they want to do—
and the key word is *do*.

Another secret is cultivating desire over discipline.
For many of us, all our lives, discipline has been associated with punishment or as a way to describe doing
what we didn't want to do. Now that we are grown, why
would we want to focus on discipline? Why would we
want to make it a large part of our life goal? Of course,
for the results that being disciplined in behavior can
bring us, but I want to look at achieving the same results
from a different approach.

Instead of thinking, "I want to be disciplined
enough to get up an hour earlier to put in work on my
side project," try thinking, "I want to work on my side
project so much that I will get up an hour earlier." It's a
tiny tweak in language choice, but it can work wonders
on your psyche. We subconsciously and consciously
resist what we find unappealing, so if you see the idea
of discipline as negative—even when intellectually you
know it's positive—then drop that word from your
mindset and focus on desire.

After all, if you are reading this book, you likely desire to be more productive at your chosen craft. This is an easy mental hack to try. Do more of what you want, and don't worry about being disciplined.

THE PROCESS, NOT THE RESULT

The fundamental component of becoming a producer is learning to love the process more than the result. So many people get caught up in spending too much time envisioning what they want. You have to know what you want and what you are after, but the only way through the disappointments and long days and thoughts of wanting to quit, is to like what you are *doing.*

If you don't have this element, then your imagined goal can never be achieved soon enough and likely never will. This is one of the biggest reasons people quit—they are looking at their journey from a *want or lack* rather than a calm assurance of *doing and being.* If you think too much about what you are *not,* that is where you'll live, and peace and accomplishments will be delayed indefinitely.

That's not to say that success can't be achieved from places of revenge, competition, or pure distaste for current circumstances. I believe people can experience success from those starting points. But I argue that finding something you enjoy doing is going to be more useful than just making enough money to get out, or to succeed in proving someone wrong, etc.

Life lived from lack or anger still rings shallow at the end. It comes short of peace because essentially you are doing it for someone other than yourself. Once you prove yourself to someone else or you beat someone else, you make more money than someone else, what's next? What's driving you?

Keep your mind right—learn to steer your thoughts.

You would have to pick another battle to engage in or an offense to feel in order to produce at that level again. At any rate, when you are consistently looking at what you think you should be or should have accomplished or hope to accomplish or want to be, etc., it puts you at a psychological disadvantage.

Keep your mind right, it's the key to the whole game, not just with productivity but with everything in life. Keep your head right and work through negativity, doubt, procrastination, fear, distraction. The mind moves a million miles an hour, one second here and the next second somewhere else. Learn to steer your thoughts and there's no limit to the amount of work you can complete.

PRODUCTIVITY THROUGH PATIENCE

Maximum productivity is more mental than physical. It is about mixing patience and grace with action and persistence. Balancing these ideas in a way that allows you to remain in an optimal mental space to work is the way to overcome distraction and create the lifestyle you want. How does patience, for example, affect productivity?

We want things to happen now, and when they don't (as of course they won't), we become discouraged. We return to a mental framework of dissatisfaction and lack in regard to our current circumstances. This leads to us being blinded to the resources that are readily available to continue doing our work—the work necessary to change our current circumstances.

So we quit. We decide that it was a bad idea or an idea that we could follow through on "When we have more time." We decide what we were doing wasn't really working after all. Whatever the excuse we make in this situation, it was likely that we just needed to deploy patience—patience with our ideas, attitudes, and results. Patience, as a mindset, is what we need to fall in love with the process. Patience allows us to wait for the ideas and be ready to accept them and put them into action when they come—but not force them or try to will them into existence to the point of frustration and failure.

When we are patient, we are open to wisdom and inspiration and ideas. All of this will give us the fuel to sustain action—when it is time to act. Patience allows us to experience each step of the process through to completion without abandoning our work due to hurry.

It's hard to force concentration. You have to let go and sink into the process in order to concentrate. Distraction is easy. It is recommended, sold, given away, and is so attractive. Concentration is rare. Try not to constantly check your progress, whether that is sales numbers, word count, interest payment, likes, subscribers, or any other measurement of results. Do more work instead. If it motivates you to keep the results in front of you, then good, but try not to check out of habit, boredom, or procrastination.

People are searching instead of awakening, looking for something that isn't instead of observing what is, hoping for instead of recognizing and being thankful for and living out of the now, out of this moment—the only one we have. When you live out of this space, it makes it easy to keep producing and keep moving forward because you don't have a choice.

HOW DO YOU VIEW LIFE?

Face each day with a chosen mentality. It comes down to how you view life. If life to you is just a storm of trying to avoid falling behind on your bills, mortgage, responsibilities at your job, your personal life, your family, and if you're just trying to stay ahead of the tax collector, etc., you won't be able to see life from a proper perspective. You are caught up in focusing on life as problems. Bend your mind. Almost anything is possible if you can overcome boredom and fear.

From the broader spectrum of millennials and ages and epochs, the 50-to-100-year human life is a blink of an eye, our successes but a flash in the pan. But the human life experienced, as it is for us, rarely seems so short. For us, it's eternity and everything matters deeply due to our experience of emotions such as love, jealousy, anger, happiness, ecstasy, and so on. It matters to us so much that we have to consciously choose positive thoughts over negative ones to avoid being constantly offended or to be conscious and exercise restraint when it comes to seeking and experiencing what we call pleasure. As a result of these emotions and the world of competition and superficiality—consumption for its own sake and shallow rewards—it's tempting to take a cynical outlook on the experience of life.

See life as the miracle it is.

It's a fair choice, but not a helpful one if you are trying be a producer. If you are trying to build something that lasts, something that you are proud of, something you can be obsessed with doing for years, then you have to see life as the miracle it is. Try to see life as if you are a child seeing an amusement park for the very first time. It's easy if you try.

Look at the objects you take for granted and notice things about them that you did not before. If you get into the habit of really looking at the objects and events happening around you on a daily basis, you'll begin to appreciate them and to look forward to waking up and going to work in the morning, or going out to sell your wares and drum up business. The internet and smart phones are amazing! We are so incredibly lucky to have been born into this world at this time.

Patience and execution are the keys. Once you see life with this perspective a time or two, you realize how it plays out. The same goes for building and finishing something. You are familiar with the feelings and the problems. You remember the feelings, problems, reactions, motivations, doubts, pressure, habits and inclinations, imagination, the good, the bad, and the ugly—you remember it all and you know it will be alright if you just keep chipping away.

PRODUCE, DON'T WORK

Maybe you say your work—your nine-to-five, your warehouse job, whatever—is the problem. If it weren't for your day job, you would be able to accomplish more and go after your dreams. This is a perfect example of why you need to start producing instead of working.

What do I mean by this? Am I saying to quit your job to start a creative endeavor? No, I'm not saying that. What I mean is, you have to spin your perspective on the whole job idea. There are so many negative connotations attached to "work."

Decide that you are whatever you wish to be and start producing. It doesn't matter if you work at a machine shop, warehouse, or an insurance office. You could even be a highly paid executive at a Fortune 500 company. If you would rather be a taxidermist, a seamstress, or a film director, the first step is to stop thinking of yourself as the person with a job at the insurance company and start producing. I know you have other things going on in your life, but what are you? A insurance salesperson or the painter that you would rather be? If you are a painter, paint!

You have to produce. If you are in your chosen career, but you would like to see more results, more financial benefits, etc., the answer again is to produce. I know that sounds oversimplified, but it's not. We have to remember that if someone else has done it in our field, then it is possible. Think it's impossible to hit the high numbers your sales manager has set for you as goals? It's not; if someone in the past has hit those numbers, you can too.

Start building your legacy today.

Whatever your career or field, if you can find a person who has done what you want to do, then you can do it too. Don't sell yourself short. The main thing is to figure out how to produce. How can you do more to get you closer to your goal? Eventually, you will make *doing* the goal and that is the hack that allows people to be productive at an extraordinary level over prolonged periods of time. When your "work" becomes habitual, you've won.

We have to get rid of this idea that there is some secret, some perfect moment in time for us to begin or to become what we want to be. That time is now. The secret is producing. Make something. Start building your legacy today, whether you think it matters in the long run or not, you'll find a more satisfactory life in creating something each day. Each day, through achieving your goals, you will be putting together the pieces of something bigger. But you have to show up and decide to build it.

12-HOUR DAYS AT WORK

Some of the most unproductive individuals spend many hours at work. The market doesn't care how long you worked, or what time you showed up and what time you left. The market cares if you produce value for the company or the business in which you find yourself. The market cares if you have a quality product to sell that will add value. The old-school idea of the number of hours you spend at work equaling work ethic and production is dying. Time will always be used as a measurement, of course, as consultants charge a certain amount per hour or per day, but they are only worth the money because of the value they offer within that time. You are paying for the value.

This being said, if you think in terms of time spent working on your goal, you may be missing the mark as well. For example, if you think setting aside two hours a day outside of your day job will be enough to get you where you want to go, well, maybe, but you might be wrong. It's best to let go of the idea of time if you can. Once you realize just how much time is actually available, you can work yourself out of the constraints of the idea and start focusing on doing what you want to do more often. It's that simple. When we focus on the time itself—how little there is, how many hours left in the day, etc.—that is when we lose focus on the work and give more strength to the limiting idea of time.

There is something to the idea of time, but not equating time with actual production. Time spent should be less important than tangible value and results. Make producing value your goal rather than working a specific amount of time.

THE POWER OF MAKING LISTS

Never underestimate the power of making lists and checking off or crossing out tasks as you complete them. I realize this can be taken to extremes and people get stuck on the making lists part, having multiple lists lying around without getting much done because they're always making lists. But if you don't already do this and you want to become more productive, this is an excellent tool.

Make your list each day either at night for the next day, or in the morning for the day ahead. Write out your tasks in as much detail as needed and mark the priority tasks as the ones that must be done first, for sure by the end of the day, or however you need to designate them to make sure the priorities are noted.

But if you don't get everything done for whatever reason, move the remaining tasks to the next day's list and if necessary put them a little closer to top of the priority list. Don't beat yourself up if you don't complete your day's list. Keep trying. Make a new list for the next day and start again.

Another hack for working through overwhelming feelings when you look at your list is to put another piece of paper on top of it and slide it down so it only reveals the top-listed task. When you complete this task, cross it out and slide the top paper down to show the next task. Not only is this effective in helping you focus only on the task at hand, it also adds to the rewarding feeling of crossing off tasks when you start to see the completed ones pile up while moving your paper down to reveal the next one. This is a mental trigger of pleasurable feelings that cause you to want to do more.

CONSEQUENCES OF REGRET

Understand the consequences of not getting it done. Really own the fear of what you'll feel in three months, or whatever your timeline is for your goal, if you do not do these things you know you *should* do. The things you know you *can* do. The things you know you *want* to do.

Again, this is a mental trick. We are conditioned to avoid feelings of displeasure, so when we are able to experience those feelings in our mind, our subconscious will remember them and we will work hard to complete our tasks and save ourselves from the feelings of regret and disappointment. It can be a real motivator to think of the consequences of not taking advantage of these moments we call time.

SCHEDULE IT!

How many times have you said, "We should get together sometime," or "I need to call someone about this project," etc., but you never get around to it? Putting a reminder into your digital calendar or physical calendar is a must for staying on schedule and completing your goals.

Remember, much of this is about freeing up mental capacity to produce more. If you are constantly thinking of appointments you need to keep or phone calls that need to be made, you are using up valuable real estate in your mind.

Put it on the calendar and into your schedule and you won't spend as much time thinking about it until it is necessary.

NO MORE WAITING

Don't make the mistake of waiting for a specific idea before beginning work on your goals. When you start working on your goal regardless of your inspiration or motivation at the time, you will find that the ideas eventually come to you. Not always, but often. Knowing this, keep attacking your work because it is possible that today is the day that the ideas will come faster than you can keep up with them.

The more you produce and create, the more ideas will come.

One of those ideas, just one is all you need to break the world wide open for you. But you never would know or see it if you didn't come to work even when you felt nothing good. That's why it is important to keep trying, no matter what. You think you need more ideas, more style, talent, ability, persistence, education, research, etc., when all you really need is a bit more courage.

Courage? Yes, the courage to work when you are not inspired.

THOUGHTS FOLLOW ACTION

We imagine that our actions are dictated by our thoughts and attitude, but is it possible that it is the other way around? Is it possible that our actions dictate who we are, who we become, and even what we think about ourselves? If this is so, it means less thinking and more doing is the way to success. It means that if we want to be a certain type of person, all we have to do is stop thinking and start being. It means that our actions are easier completed when we don't think about them, because our thoughts are relegated to our earlier actions, which may not have been what we wanted. If we want to change, we need to change our actions and our thoughts will follow. It creates a feedback loop.

This explains the reason those rare people are able to produce at levels that don't really make sense. They started doing the things they imagined without over-thinking them first. After doing, they began to think like the person they were acting as. And even when the action they took led to poor results or undesirable consequences, they didn't revert to their earlier self and decide they had failed, they thought like their new self and figured out a solution or learned from their mistake.

Action leads to thinking that supports the action.

Action—taking action leads to thinking that accompanies or supports that action. This is how people produce like crazy, they act like what they want to be. If you are a writer and you want to be prolific like Isaac Asimov (who wrote or edited more than 500 books) in terms of output, you sit down and you write. We tend to complicate things and imagine a system that will completely revolutionize the way we approach work. Or perhaps, we think of someone like Asimov as a teacher, someone who has learned something that we don't know or have yet to learn. But it's simple.

The answer is in the action itself. If you want to sell like the world's greatest salesperson, get out there and sell. It's not hard to get a sales job, but it's hard to make money at it if you aren't good. Get a sales job and sell. You learn everything you can along the way, you sell, you work, you act like the person you want to be. Eventually your mind follows suit. You start seeing the world differently. You start looking for opportunities. Not looking per say, but observing them—seeing them for the first time even though they've been around you all this time. You just keep working harder than you did before because you are not who you were before. You do all those things that you wanted to do before, and you do them more quickly than you imagined.

CONTENTMENT THROUGH WORK

"Always you have been told that work is a curse and labour a misfortune. But I say to you that when you work you fulfil a part of earth's furthest dream, assigned to you when that

> dream was born, and in keeping
> yourself with labour you are in
> truth loving life, and to love life
> through labour is to be intimate
> with life's inmost secret."
>
> —KHALIL GIBRAN,
> author of *The Prophet*

When you are working on what you love and what you are good at, you are being who you are. This is essentially the answer to a lot of what we mistakenly seek elsewhere. The peace and contentment that we seek in external sources—like more money, bigger houses, different places to live, and new relationships and religions—can be found inside. When we are doing our work, we live and exist outside of time and our ego, allowing for a feeling of complete fulfillment whether we notice it or not. When we are in tune, we don't notice anything but the work we are doing in the moment.

The longer we sustain that feeling, the more contentment we experience and this becomes our goal.

FINDING YOUR GROOVE

When you are mentally prepared to produce, once you get there, you sink into the details, the nitty gritty, the process. Remember that when you do get into the groove, oftentimes the mind will attack you with everything it's got. The ego will try to get you out of your zone or prevent you from falling into it—it wants your attention on you, not your work. So be prepared for thoughts about guilt and resentment and everything in between. Work slowly through these periods. Slowly, lightly, methodically, get work done in the face of your demons. And then say to yourself, *Today was a good day.*

But what about the days when you don't get into that groove? What about when you don't get much done and you don't find a rhythm of work due to interruptions or a stream of negative thoughts? How do you get out of a production slump?

In the next chapter, we'll look at some ways to motivate yourself even when you don't want to be motivated.

CHAPTER 5

MOTIVATE YOURSELF

Motivation doesn't always come to you on command, but if you're patient, it will come. Sure as the night follows the day. And when it does, you won't want to stop working. This is experiential in nature and it may sound obvious. It may be an idea you've heard a hundred times before, but if you want to be more productive and you aren't able to generate your own motivation, wait.

Let the muse come to you, don't go to the muse. She won't be found. She's attracted to you when you are sitting down and doing your work, especially when you are depressed and out of sorts and full of self-loathing and existential blues. That's when motivation sneaks up and gives you some sort of superhuman strength to make time disappear and cause your mind to connect with your goals and your work and the muse comes with inspiration and ideas—and hours later, you realize the time that has passed. But you have to be at work, you can't give up.

Don't make the mistake of thinking you must feel motivated to do what you need to do, you don't. You only need to start. Think of it as getting out of bed when you don't want to. Swing your feet over the side and place them on the floor. Showing up is often the part of the process that we resist the most; and in a way, it's the easiest part to overcome. Just show up and start the task. Start. Let the motivation come when it comes.

STIMULATE DESIRE

Fan the flame of creativity and production. Stimulate your desire to produce. This stimulus can come in many forms and through many methods of triggering. Ideally, it is just pure excitement about the project you are working on that causes you to look forward to putting in as much time as you can—as soon as you can—and for as long as you can.

But, of course, there are ups and downs in life. Feelings, emotions, unfortunate events, and just the overall cyclical nature of motivation means that sometimes you will have to learn how to cause yourself to do the work when you don't want to.

Another way to do this is to flip the negative perspective of demotivated feelings into a positive by using the stress to fuel your work. So when you are feeling overwhelmed about something outside of your goal-related work—maybe it's relationship stress, financial stress, or daily work stress—use your goal-related project as an escape, an outlet, a distraction from that stress. Not all distraction is negative.

It might seem counterintuitive, and some might argue that you should immediately face that stressful situation head-on, but try this out. It can really motivate you to produce and make progress, which lessens your anxiety and opens your mind and actually creates a better, stronger mindset with which to face that other problem or stressor.

TGIF

Sometimes you might not feel motivated on Mondays or Tuesdays or in the morning or during other times that people might traditionally be working. That's okay. Work when others are taking it easy. Work during the weekend if you can.

Holidays and weekends are not times for feeling depressed or overly celebratory—these are perfect times to work. Take advantage of the time when the rest of society is sitting still. Depressed on the holidays? Here's a solution: produce, work, hustle. Put in work and forget about the holidays.

I'm not telling people with families to ignore them. It has to be practical within your individual situation, but if you typically party on weekends or on the holidays or if you feel low during those times because you are lonely, or perhaps you have a partner who would support you if you chose to work during these times, choose to work. Know your situation and pay attention to this opportunity. It's a massive chance to get ahead and feel better.

Start looking forward to weekends for a different reason.

So you went out with friends last night, you had too much to drink and now you're paying for it. Or maybe you had too much caffeine throughout the day and didn't get good sleep that night. You wake up feeling groggy with a headache and ready to lay back down. Or maybe you feel fine until you can't find anything to wear or you realize you are out of something you need or your car won't start, etc. Ride these times out and allow the remainder of the day to potentially be productive.

Don't give up on a day because of the morning.

Even if you have to go to bed early that night to make up for the past night, do it. Don't just lay in bed and watch movies and read books all day—unless you're truly ill, of course. Don't let yourself give in to feeling badly. Get up and push through the rough mornings knowing you've done it before. Get back into your work—your project, your next sale doesn't care how you feel. Start working and you'll be surprised how you forget about that headache or that lack of sleep.

Maybe you wake up feeling great...until you get an angry voicemail, text, or email from a coworker, business associate, or a client the second you start working. Work through it. Take it with a grain of salt because you know it will pass, and the rest of the day can be productive if you don't hold on to the negativity.

Many amazing days have started with dreadful mornings. Don't give up on the day until it's done.

SWITCH IT UP BETWEEN PROJECTS

Usually we have more than one goal or project to complete. Even if it is a long-term goal, it often requires many different smaller scale projects to be completed in order to get there. Switch back and forth between those projects and goals. If you get bored with one or reach a standstill, get into the other one. Just be careful not to get into different projects that actually compete with each other.

Another opportunity would be with your personal life and your professional life. Maybe you have a great day at work and you feel good about your level of productivity—channel that energy into the project at home that you've started but have been unable to finish. Sometimes that good energy will transfer into productivity on home or personal projects, too. Otherwise, it can be vice versa. You can have a lousy day of production at work yet get a ton of personal work done like having a fantastic workout or run.

While it can be detrimental to have too many things going at once, it can also be helpful so long as you are practiced at closing. When you know you will finish each project, it can be a tremendous benefit to have something else to go to when you are stuck on one. It allows the mind to refocus on the second project while opening up for ideas to take shape in the background for the first project—the one you took a break from.

LAUGH AT YOURSELF

Bertrand Russell pointed out that the sign of an oncoming nervous breakdown is taking one's work terribly seriously. We need to be able to laugh at ourselves and enjoy humor and see that no work is so important that it should cause us pain and stress in our personal lives. Our minds create unwarranted anxiety.

When we are unmotivated or feeling poorly about what we've not accomplished, we are judging ourselves too harshly. It's our ego claiming its feelings of self-importance and making life seem to be far more serious than the experience really is. Take a step back and laugh at the situation.

FAILING BRINGS POWER

If you are feeling unmotivated due to a recent failure, consider the following perspective: no one sets out to fail, but it happens. When you fail, usually it means you are trying to do something. Other times, failure can be out of your control—fire, flood, car accident, a supporting business that folds, etc.—but typically it is when you are working to make something happen. This is better than not trying and not failing.

Regardless of the reason for the failure, if you get back up and try again, you put yourself in a stronger position to succeed than before. Maybe that seems wrong to you. Maybe you had more money to work with before you failed or a better office or home or the support of a now-lost loved one.

Whatever your loss and failure, power is generated in the effort to rise again and be productive. There is a strength gained that you did not previously have access to. If you fail, try again and you will see that this is true. Never stop or quit on some goal due to failure. You'll miss out on the greatest times of productivity and energy and achievement that you could imagine.

PRODUCE WHAT YOU CONSUME

Producing what you consume is a guiding ideal that can motivate you when you are feeling low. It is one that has the power to change your life. As you start making your own way, creating more of your own lifestyle, you can notice a significant change in the number of others' lifestyles and philosophies that you consume. And this in turn will not only make you happier, it will make you more productive.

When you find yourself scrolling through Instagram posts for hours, prompt yourself to create a couple of your own. When you read blogs every morning, whether they are inspirational and good for you or not, start a plan to set up your own blog and contribute to the conversation. It's a way of thinking that will get you into productive habits.

What can you produce around your strengths? What do you know and live that you could package for others who would benefit from its creation?

This is a fairly simple one to measure and you may find that you enjoy the creation of a product even more than the consumption depending on what it is. But the point is to look around and notice all of the opportunities for you to create or package something that would help others if it were put out into the world in consumable form.

We keep too much to ourselves. Make something today that can help impact someone tomorrow. It can be as small as an Instagram post or a card or a word of encouragement sent via text message. The inspiration is all around you, if you take the time to notice.

"However, for the man who studies to gain insight, books and studies are merely rungs of the ladder on which he climbs to the summit of knowledge. As soon as a rung has raised him up one step, he leaves it behind. On the other hand, the many who study in order to fill their memory do not use the rungs of the ladder for climbing, but take them off and load themselves with them to take away, rejoicing at the increasing

weight of the burden. They remain below forever, because they bear what should have borne them."
—ARTHUR SCHOPENHAUER

DON'T THINK, JUST DO

The more you think, the more likely you will be to talk yourself out of doing what you need to do. Be too busy to think about it too much. If you follow this modus operandi, things will work themselves out because you are in alignment with the universe by doing what you are supposed to be doing. Be too busy doing what you were meant to do.

Don't spend time researching advice and guidance on personal issues. Too much stock is being placed in other people's experiences. Have your own. Work and enjoy family time when you get it. Then work hard. I don't mean work hard in the physical sense (although it could mean this), but hard as in intensely focused on the work of your choosing. If you want to do or be something, work hard at making it happen.

Don't let your mind drift off to unresolved conflict or paranoid thoughts or anything that is negative to your spirit. It will bring you down. Instead, let your mind be still and let it sink into the task at hand. Contentment and ease from your anxiety will follow.

There is a difference between just "doing something" and doing work that brings you closer to your goals. If you are just moving to move—motion without goals—then you're missing the introspective part of this altogether.

THE WINTERTIME BLUES

If you live in an area like North America where there are long winters, you know just what the phrase "wintertime blues" means. It's the time of year when it seems like it's been cold and dark, rainy or icy or snowy for the last year and a half, and you can barely remember what summer and spring feels like. You feel depressed and sluggish and pale.

You've eaten too much and exercised too little over the past four months, and you lack the energy to start changing your ways. Plus, it looks miserable outside. Productivity dips to an all-time low, you are slow to address problems; emails and phone calls just keep getting pushed to the back burner. Welcome to the worst time of the year.

There is a way to beat this emotion when you feel it. Ride with it. Sit with it. Feel it. Don't try to overcome it. Let it take its course—be at peace with negative feelings. You are not lazy. You just feel lazy and external influences are affecting this. Don't be concerned with your numbers. It's a losing game to do so. You won't be satisfied, and you shouldn't be as you know your energy level will be below the standards of productivity you have set for yourself.

Try to do nothing. Sit and stare into space. Look out the window and peer deeply into the universe. This sounds weird, but the results are not. You will find your mind growing quiet, and you'll notice a slowing or a halt to the ceaseless chatter in your mind about what you need to do. You'll realize that almost everybody you know is feeling the same way and the universe and people and energy are connected, and there is no need to get angry.

There is no need to judge yourself and beat yourself up about the way you've been slacking. There's no need to be upset with your colleague. There's simply no need. Just eat, sleep, and take care of your responsibilities the best way you can today. You will realize it is all you really need.

As your mind empties, a funny thing happens. You start to feel ideas arising and you begin to act on them. You act without thinking too much. Before long, you pick up that book you started reading three months ago and you find motivating, inspirational content. You start writing again. You pick up the phone. You come back to the sales floor with renewed vigor, ready to talk to people.

It's okay to be still, to sit and stare off into the distance. You don't always have to be working; empty your mind so it can draw in more ideas, creativity, and inspiration. Learn to still the mind and accept peaceful periods of doing nothing.

OUTPRODUCE YOUR PROBLEMS

The alternative to accepting that low feelings will pass is to outwork your feelings. Here's what I mean:

When you are working, achieving, and producing, you notice your problems less. They seem distant. You don't hear high-level achievers complaining about their problems even though you know they have them just like everyone else. This is because they understand that no one really cares that much. What people care about is production. You want people to care? Be a producer, make something happen, do something and become obsessed with it. Fall in love with doing it better and more often than you did yesterday.

Today will be better!

When you get into this mindset, today will always be better than yesterday. But the great thing is that you will be too busy to compare the two. Today will always be the priority, the focus, the next big to-do. Even if the day turns out to be a wash and you get nothing accomplished that you wanted, you will say the next morning when you wake up, "Today will be better." It's a call to action. It's the call of your soul or spirit or true self—whatever you want to name it, it is that inner voice telling you to do the thing you want to do. And before you know it, you've had one of the most productive days of your life.

Problems? What are your problems, right now? I mean right this second—what is your problem?

You'll always have some issue or another, but when you are working, they all go away. For those moments you no longer have problems and that is the space you can learn to operate from. This is not advice to run from your problems, but to outproduce them. Make them smaller by concentrating on your work. You will feel much more calm and able to face and diagnose a problem after you have completed a day of work and massive production.

Learn how to use your ability to sustain work for long periods of time to your advantage. If you are doing what you want, it will not drain you, it will recharge you.

ACCEPT WHAT IS

The great genius of producers, creators, and achievers is not inherent most of the time. Instead, it is a practiced ability to recognize and accept what is. They don't think about what should be, could be, or needs to be done differently in order for them to succeed at what they do. They see what is and then they are able to act accordingly.

This mentality allows successful people to do what they *want* to do, not what they *should* do, and this becomes the difference between producers and those who admire them, consume their products, and follow

their careers. It's an obvious distinction between producers and consumers. Consumers are bored and
looking for something to fix the situation because they
don't accept the present reality. They are always searching. This is the opportunity for the achiever. Make
something happen with what is and stop focusing on
what should be.

Focus on what is, not on what should be.

Do what you want more and more and keep moving on toward your goal. There is nothing else you
should be doing—no circumstances under which you
could be doing better, it's just now with who you are
and what you've got.

Trust that there will be situations in which you
are not happy with yourself or your output. You will
be tempted to judge yourself and label yourself, but
let this temptation pass and get back to work as soon
as you can. Even if you feel you've wasted time or

opportunities due to failing, keep coming back to the truth of what is. That is, you are a high-level achiever, mover, and producer.

Don't let that fall from your mind. Grasp this and you will be nearly invincible. Only death will completely halt your production.

Always be adjusting to your circumstances. Even if you are working around difficult people or people who don't "get it," you can still produce. Work within the confines of your current situation, and if need be, work to get out. But always work and recognize aspects of people, politics—the culture of where you are— and negotiate your way through to do more of what you want.

You'll not get out of it by fighting and resisting, you'll get out through your work—the work that you choose and want to do. It's a simple concept, but not always simple in action. It takes time, but time passes anyway, so use it to observe and notice opportunities that can potentially provide personal growth or bring you closer to your ultimate goal.

What can you do more of right now that would potentially bring you closer to your goal?

I'M GOING TO COUNT TO THREE...!

Remember being a child and hearing this line? "I'm going to count to three and..." It meant certain consequences if you didn't do what you were supposed to do by the time your parent counted to three. This psychological sense of urgency was exaggerated by the countdown.

Try it on yourself as an adult. Count backward from five and then begin doing whatever activity you were delaying yourself from doing. If you are postponing sending an email, count backward from five and then compose and send the email. Or if it's a phone call or a conversation, count down and then do it. It's strange, but for some reason it works on your psyche; and after you do it a couple of times, you will start pattern-recognizing the countdown and automatically get ready to get into action when you start counting down.

This is part of a larger strategy of giving yourself deadlines by which to accomplish your goals. Try, with each and every one of them, to assign a deadline for completion. This is not only a good way to motivate yourself if you are a procrastinator by nature, it also can help you schedule work more effectively. Use a digital calendar to record your deadlines for each goal and any important steps in a project or process.

WHAT ENERGIZES YOU AND WHAT BRINGS YOU DOWN?

What do you dread or what makes you uncomfortable about your work. Is it attending meetings? Conducting employee evaluations? Phone calls? Having to manage financial records? What parts of your work frustrate you or cause you to feel tired afterward?

On the opposite side of this coin, think about what you love doing in your work. Is it negotiating a business deal? Making the sale? Meeting your quota? Analyzing numbers and finding the story within? Managing daily tasks and production? Think about what you do in your work that causes you to lose track of time and forget your worries and problems—because you are enjoying doing the work.

These two sets of information are important for a couple of reasons. One, knowing what you dread tells you what you need to delegate and outsource as much as possible. Double down on your strengths and try to spend less time on the activities that drain your energy. You will see your productivity increase by making these adjustments according to your self-analysis.

Two, knowing what you love to do tells you what sort of work in general you are going to be successful at or are already successful at performing, and what you need to do more of.

HANG AROUND PEOPLE WHO MOTIVATE YOU TO DO MORE

When I say "hang around," it doesn't have to mean in person as in your family or coworkers, etc. Think about the people you might hang around via the internet, through books, or TV. Think about who provides much of the content you consume. Which authors' books do you like to read? What kind of audio books do you listen to?

Make sure hang out with people who motivate you to do more, plain and simple. Many people motivate others to *buy* more or *want* more without motivating them to *do* more. Watch for this.

In my case, I used to read material by writers with pessimistic outlooks and philosophies. I enjoyed thinking and discovering the ways in which I had been deceived in my upbringing and education as well as by media and advertising. It was freeing. It allowed me to see things differently and with less delusion. But as I continued to consume this information past the point of usefulness, I noticed my attitude grew dark and paranoia and disappointment became more present in my life. I had to let go of many favorite authors and content creators due to the fact that their material did not motivate me to do more.

These are people we "hang around" whether physically or not. If their words and actions influence you, make sure it is in a positive way.

A lot of this comes back to letting go. Once you have learned your lesson, you don't need to keep going back to the teacher. It's time for you to go out and do, and eventually you may become a teacher yourself, passing along what you've learned to others who can go out and fulfill their destiny. It's great to consume interesting and creative material from people who are skilled at presenting it, but if it is not helping you do more, find the people and content that does.

CHOOSE YOUR WORDS

Controlling our language is, in a way, controlling our emotions. When you think about how often or think of the ways in which our emotion drives our talking, it can be observed that we lose control of the words we say when we lose control of our emotions.

This is not always in anger, frustration, or sadness. Examples of this can be seen when we are overly excited, anticipatory, and victorious. Sometimes we are simply feeling euphoric and stimulated and say too many words too fast. Talking more and faster is not the way to be more productive in most cases. That's not to say that if you are blessed with the gift of gab that it is negative to your production, any salesperson will tell you that's not true.

It is to say that when you choose those words with care, when you listen just a little bit more often than you talk, you will be given ideas and insight that can really increase your production in ways you never would have thought possible. Remember, it is okay to be silent. Not all silence must be awkward. Wait, and choose your words carefully when in conversations with others.

USE EMOTION

Especially anger and frustration can be used to dial in to concentrated effort and be extremely productive. We have the urgent, pressing need to be right, especially when our ego is offended and we are hurt. It's as if we believe we can enact justice—but we can't; and even being right won't change anything really. Just do more work. When you are upset and hurt and you think that all is unfair, do more. Go into your workshop, your laptop, your phone, and work.

It may not be the answer you wanted, but it's the answer you seek. No other course of action will be better and time heals. Get something done and feel better in the morning. Life goes on as it always has and always will. Don't take your particular hurt feelings and emotions of anger as so important to think that the universe cares. It doesn't, the energy will only reflect your negative energy and it will spread and bounce back and you will not feel better for being right.

Emotions are fickle indicators of the truth, a flimsy excuse for your behavior. Learn to act despite emotions. Don't react to people's words; but when it does happen that someone gets under your skin, try to bottle it up until you can uncork it into your work.

ONE PIECE AT A TIME

How do you eat an elephant? Not that you would want to, but this is the essence of the one piece at a time truth of production. The imagery captures the idea that the *only* way to get it done is one bite at a time. You might want it to be done all at once, and when you get started, you will experience times when you wish it would go more quickly, but the production process can only be completed by accomplishing all the little steps one after another.

This is something to be experienced rather than something that is simply repeated and understood from afar. When you put together a puzzle or a model airplane or sew a quilt, patience and persistence are the keys. It doesn't happen fast, it happens in moments, actions, in separate sequences rather than a burst of production. Living this philosophy over time allows us to approach goal-setting and productivity with the correct mindset. Practicality brings progress.

Practice focusing on the one piece that you are working on in this moment. It is easy to get discouraged by looking at everything that needs to be done. Avoid the temptation to look too far ahead.

CHAPTER 6

COMPLETE, EVALUATE, AND BEGIN AGAIN

T his is the hard part—finishing one part of your work to begin another; following through to completion with your goals; finishing one project and letting go of it and the results.

Letting go is often difficult when you've been involved in a creative endeavor or a consistent effort to reach certain sales goals. When you are involved in a process for a long period of time and you go through ups and downs and obstacles and inspiration, to suddenly consider that process complete is like saying goodbye to a close friend.

We fight this letting go in many ways. Sometimes, we tell ourselves that our work is not good enough. Other times, we say that it will be good enough with a bit more work. Still other times, we fear the criticism and opinions of others that could come with being done with a project and putting it out into the world. Maybe you are on the brink of selling a company that you built and you are at the negotiating table and you fear the reaction to the price you will ask.

There is another temptation that rears its head when you are close to finishing, but not quite there. This is the desire to rest, to take it easy and relish the fact that you are almost done. After all that work, you are almost done! *The deal is as good as closed. Might as well take the night off and work on finishing it up this weekend.* Somehow or another, our minds start conflating "almost finished" with finished. This weekend becomes next weekend, and many of us are inclined to even begin another project as if we were in fact done with the previous set of goals. The mind is powerful in its deception.

Be aware of these aspects of closing the deal, finishing the work, and putting the product out there. Make sure you finish.

DON'T LET PERFECTIONISM STALL YOU

Learn to let go of even of your own opinion and feelings about what you're working on when it is time to close the deal. We get stalled on work that should be finished because of our insecurities or our desire to have everything just right. We hang on to it and keep working on it long past the point of being productive, and this begins to inhibit us from moving on to the next project or taking the next step in the process.

When you know that you will always find more fault with your work than anyone else, you can find that line between good and perfect and abandon the project there. Otherwise, you won't get it done; and if you don't get it done, you won't get the next one done, or the next one.

This doesn't mean being sloppy and rushing through everything and shipping low-quality products or services, but it does mean being conscious of your own tendencies and moderating them in order to move forward.

SECOND-GUESSING

Second-guessing becomes more prominent the closer you get to finishing. The mind goes into overdrive working to convince you that what you are doing is not going to be well-received, a waste of time. Other things will have an appeal that they never had before as they distract you from finishing—it's as if they glow with attraction. It could be another idea that comes to mind, or another contact that you made through networking that could be the next big sale. These are distractions right now.

While you're working, ignore the moments where you second-guess yourself. It's nothing more than doubt that invites fear so your lizard brain can use it as a reason to quit. And if you give your ego an inch, it'll take a mile and before you know it, anxious feelings will end your productivity.

If you feel doubt creeping in, ignore it and keep working. You can work the doubt right out of your system and life. When you are dissatisfied about something, the solution is to work more.

Giving in to doubt about abilities, direction, or any other variable might be the king of production killers. Crush that doubt by working through it until you don't hear it anymore. When I worked as a project manager at a media company, a wise man by the name of D.G. Wild once taught me it's important to continue whether you are in doubt or not, because it's worse to not make a decision or to delay it too long than to make the wrong decision. Keep moving!

ACCOUNTABILITY

Make yourself accountable to someone you respect. Give the person a deadline for yourself to finish whatever it is you are finishing. Otherwise, you may not notice how much time goes by. We don't know the potential ramifications of our procrastination until there is nothing we can do about it. It's too late. And there's nothing worse than too late as poet and prolific writer Charles Bukowski observed years ago, "There are worse things than being alone but it often takes decades to realize this and most often when you do it's too late and there's nothing worse than too late."

When you put yourself out there in this way, your ego won't allow you to miss that deadline. Or at least not for long. If you tell people you are going to do something by a certain date and you don't, you lose respect in their eyes and your own. Own these consequences and place that sense of urgency on yourself to complete what you are working on. Achieve your goals by making yourself accountable to someone you would not want to disappoint in this way.

DON'T FOLLOW TOO CLOSELY

When it comes to writing, I call the advice of not following too closely the Hunter Thompson effect or the Bukowski effect. There is a romanticized notion—especially in the writing world, but this is true of other fields in other ways—that creative pursuits, in this case writing, are enhanced and improved by drinking and drug use. Thompson famously attributed his drug and alcohol use as helpful in his success, but biographers point out that his production decreased in accordance with his increased substance abuse. The same was said of iconic writers F. Scott Fitzgerald and Ernest Hemingway.

It makes sense to follow others' methods to success, but don't get caught up in imitating their every nuance, habit, and inclination. Follow the more general, basic steps—which in most cases begins with, you guessed it, action. Knowing yourself is key. Don't believe something just because you want to believe it. Because someone you respect or admire is successful with a certain method or system of action, the same method does not necessarily translate into success for you. It doesn't mean you don't try it, but don't count on it always working. Keep to the basics, the universal rules and steps to success, the tried and true, time-tested paths.

In addition to this, know when to stop. There is a time when you get too tired or have passed the point of quality and you know it is time to take a break or go to sleep. Heed this call. Tomorrow is a new day full of fresh, new possibilities. You've put in a good day if you hit your goals for the day. It is possible to take it too far or do too much.

AVOID COMPARISONS

Don't compare your work or career with those of others'. The aim is to execute your own ideas. The more you start comparing yourself or your work to others—just like consuming others' ideas—the more you weaken the creativity that is uniquely yours. Other people will rise up and have their time of success if they put in the work and take advantage of opportunities. Your time will come as well.

It's okay to have friends in your industry, even if they are "competitors," to trade ideas and stories and lessons, but don't measure your production or work by theirs. They have a different story. Write your own. Measure your productivity and success by your own personal standards. *Everyone is in their own time zone.*

Create, don't compare.

Comparing yourself or the speed of your progress is a false indicator of personal growth, worth, and achievement. It leads to wasted time and eventual negativity. Create, don't compare.

MAKE YOUR STORY PRIORITY OVER YOUR BANK ACCOUNT

"In the end, we all become stories."
–MARGARET ATWOOD

Think about your story. What will people say about you after you die—how do you want to be remembered? If you care about building something of significance, make that the priority rather than going after the money in the short term. There are many opportunities for short-term financial gains that can actually hurt your long-term plans.

It's a trap to go after money instead of freeing up your time, or going after money that's easy to make but not necessarily in line with your character or desired legacy. Make sure the way you make your money is in line with your values.

EVALUATE YOUR WORK

Once you've gone through the steps just mentioned, the last step prepares you and motivates you to begin the next project, sales campaign, etc. Here is where you evaluate your work, where you look at the steps you took to completion, what you could have done differently, where you could have saved time, improved quality, etc. This analysis helps you formulate a plan for your next attempt.

Your next project will follow in line with the formula you have created, only you will learn additional hacks and improvements to the process along the way. The formula will become more refined each time you use it.

The process comes down to:

- deciding on your work,

- focusing on one area of interest or expertise,

- following the smaller goals and steps that you've planned,

- finishing every last step,

- and then evaluating the process to develop your own formula that you can use over again.

It may be more than one thing, but start with one and focus, follow through, and finish so that you can see a formula begin to take shape. When you do have this formula, the next project will likely go faster or maybe it will be more in depth, more valuable.

PRODUCTIVITY TEMPTATIONS

There are certain temptations that come with achieving levels or degrees of success in your journey. One is to romanticize the next step of your success before you have completed it. It is easy to fantasize about how it will feel or how others will react when you've accomplished that next goal or step. This is a form of overconfidence and it can be a weakness.

It's good to set the goal and stimulate thoughts through a clear vision, that burning desire to achieve, just don't get a big idea about getting bigger than the process. You're always only as good as the work you continue to do. This is important to remember as you complete, close, finish work. Don't stall out while basking in the celebration of achievement or while contemplating your next success. Nothing is promised.

Take success for granted at your own peril.

Take success for granted at your own peril. Execution is the game. Looking too long at past work or too far ahead at imagined work results in procrastination. Procrastination means lost production. Stay here in the mix and put in work on the new project, the new deal, that new connection you are establishing, that next goal. Always ask yourself, *What's next?*

Complacency is the end. Don't romanticize the work or the finished product. Just embrace and sink into the production process as life. Stay with it as long as you can and then just a bit longer. More work equals more inspiration. Don't look for starting points and ending points. Let it flow.

Don't look for what triggered a productive day that was particularly impressive to you. When you do this, you run the risk of attributing credit incorrectly. For example, it was the muse, the workout, the book, the conversation, the rub of my lucky snail statue. Then you try to replicate those circumstances and it doesn't always work out, and you are discouraged.

There are certain macro-level variables that are important to duplicate such as accepting your prime time of production—morning, midday, night—but those will only be known for sure after repeatedly trying, failing, and succeeding. After successes and failures, you will have a basic set of variables that you can follow rinse-and-repeat style. But be careful of being pulled into the notion—especially when you are starting out—that there is some source of inspiration that causes your success. There's not.

It is true that certain habits and traditions might help you. Things like having a certain type of food and sleep and beginning work at a specific time, but don't become so reliant on structure that you can't work under other different circumstances. As a rule, imagine the work coming to and through you rather than through carefully crafted circumstances.

At the end of the day, it's a blend of sources—but the main one will always be doing the work.

There's a spark of confidence you can give yourself. When you see firsthand what is possible, it propels you to push yourself even more. When you would have typically headed to bed to watch some YouTube or listen to an audio book, now you might stay involved in the work, in the process just a bit longer.

This is the magic. In fact, if there is something magical about the whole process, it is the cycle of desire, action, more action, a tiny bit of success, more action, more and more action, more success, and so on. Do it for the contentment, not the applause, and you won't be disappointed.

OUTSIDE PERSPECTIVE

The only thing we are more obsessed with than ourselves, is others' reactions to us or others' perspectives of us. Why? What is this deep connection to our ego? Why is someone's perception of us of any value? Does it really mean anything? Obviously, it means everything.

Because we can't see ourselves as the world sees us, any tangible feedback from the world is something we can learn about ourselves, the selves we can't see or understand. You can't see your own head unless from a mirror, and that is only the physical you. You need others to see and get to know you to help you see yourself through their eyes. This is useful to accept for the following reasons: First, the more you do, the more feedback you'll get. Therefore, the better you'll know yourself. The better you know yourself, the more you'll do—feedback loop.

Second, its useful to accept because you can then begin the slow process of detaching from your ego and actually get closer to that out-of-body experience that will change the way you look at reality. This too will allow you to work harder, do more, and simultaneously feel less desire for the feedback. So you'll care less about the results and more about the doing, which is the goal.

SHARING, LEARNING, STAYING OPEN

Helping others by giving them value is its own reward. It may seem cliché to say so at this point, but it's true. We make a mistake when we think everyone is out to get us, and it's nothing but a dog-eat-dog world, so anything we learn we should keep to ourselves. This kind of thinking does not help us in the long term. Even if we benefit immediately by not sharing what helps us, we lose in the long run due to lost networking opportunities and friendships and business relationships that could have led to much bigger things.

On the basic level of human psychology, we crave relationships with other people. Be a mentor to someone who has the same interest or is following a similar career path. Many of us have benefitted immensely by having people more skilled, more experienced who shared their wisdom with us and gave us guidance. You can do the same for someone even if you are not that far along in your journey of success.

Having an attitude of sharing and connecting and mentoring will do nothing but boost your productivity levels, so do not hesitate. Live with this in mind: the mental rewards you receive from helping others will give you creative energy and an increased desire to do more. It's the perfect productivity stimulus.

WORK AS AN OUTLET FOR EMOTIONS

Let your work be an outlet. Rather than drinking negative emotions away, use those emotions to benefit you.

Work as an answer to your problems will end up giving you the answers you seek elsewhere.

Memento Mori: remember your mortality. Remembering that you only have one life and that you are going to die is a tremendous motivator for some. Think of the idea of sacrificing a Friday night, a Saturday, or a weekend in order to work and accomplish what you want. Can you afford to give up a weekend that you would typically waste in nonproductive activities? How badly do you want to save money for that house or toward your own financial freedom?

SCHEDULE TIME FOR YOUR PROJECT

If you are doing something that falls outside of your normal daily grind, maybe it is a side project that you are hoping can be used as a Plan B or eventually become your Plan A to get you out of the job or career you are in now. If this is the case, and even if it isn't, schedule some time with yourself to work on this project.

Just like you would schedule and plan meetings for the work you do for someone else, set aside that time for yourself to plan, update, hold yourself accountable, and set new goals. This is an important step in getting the snowball rolling, especially early on with whatever you're doing, as you're likely to be doing it alone. And that's a good thing. Then as you build it maybe others come along, but right now, to have important meetings with yourself, the CEO of your life, is essential.

KISS

We all know this acronym—KISS—means Keep It Simple Stupid. It is natural for us to make simple things complicated, especially when it comes to processes, because it gives our ego an excuse to get out of the work. But that's the old way of looking at it. Simplify your strategy.

Don't build a plan with 200 steps in it. Don't look that far ahead, it will only slow you down. Think about what you want and break it down into the reasonable steps. If step one is research, schedule a time with yourself to do it, allot a set amount of time, and then complete it. For example, we may hung up on problems or questions we can't answer off the top of our heads, and friends or family don't know the answers either. So we procrastinate and make no progress, when all it takes is twenty minutes of research on the internet to find the solutions or answers.

So break down your plan to the most basic. Maybe the first step is just meeting yourself in your most mentally productive space, whether that's your office, car, or shower, and deciding on what you want to accomplish and what you would like to be doing on a daily basis if you could make such a decision.

FOR THE PESSIMISTS

Some people think too much. I would say some are cursed to think too much, but it typically wouldn't be considered a curse, and even in today's world, being introspective has its benefits. However, making it in the dog-eat-dog world of consumerism, hierarchy, and politics of our society is generally not a preferred situation for the philosopher or the thinker. As such, we are born into a world that many of us were not designed for.

Anxiety results. A sense of cynicism can overtake us as we stay on the sidelines and the outskirts and observe what the people playing the game can't seem to see. We see corruption being strengthened by the ideas of competition outweighing ideas of cooperation. We see the effects of advertising and media and how it benefits government and corporate power in a lopsided way. It seems immoral to be part of such a society, but we are part of it and we must decide what we will do with our lives and the situation in which we find ourselves.

THE WORLD NEEDS MORE OPTIMISTS

Choose to make something that you believe brings value to the world, to other people. Maybe it embodies some of the ideas that you believe are lacking in today's popular discourse in certain areas of society. To work hard and produce something that can help establish your own philosophy is a benefit to you and others you may not know but who are just like you—who need what you have to offer.

We need more people talking about optimism.

We need to hear your voice and what you are about. Please don't hold it in due to the pessimistic side of human nature and life. Sure there is plenty wrong with our world, but there is plenty that is right and good as well. Dwell on these things. If you already know the truth, you don't need to spend time on the websites that constantly point out the delusions of the masses or the horrible, negative actions of your country's government or the possibility that our "reality" is a simulation.

On many levels, true or not, these things are irrelevant. You were born into this world, what you choose to do is your choice. In your own personal life, you can make the choices about what you eat, what you watch, and how you earn and spend your money. Think about this when it comes to your consumption of ideas that may reinforce the evils of our world rather than consuming ideas that will improve and better the ways of the world. Think to yourself, *I have a choice to consume this again or to begin to live my life in a way that reflects my positive views and beliefs. Which choice is more useful?*

HUSTLE, NOT HASTE

"Hustle" is a popular word. It's easy to associate words like "hustle" and "grind" with speed and constant motion and results. Making your dreams and goals a reality doesn't happen quickly, and you shouldn't feel pressure to make it happen quickly. As long as you are building habits that allow you to continually get closer to the life you want to live, you are doing the right thing. Sometimes you may feel super productive, and other times little steps will be made that get you closer to your goal.

Other times, you may make giant steps yet due to their subtle nature and the place where you are on your journey, you won't even notice them. The key is to enjoy life, have fun, take everything lightly, and continue to work hard at the things you like doing—and you will find your version of success.

WORK IN CALMNESS AND SINCERITY

Make sincerity a goal in conversation and life. And it's not as though it should be a goal in and of itself. It's a way of checking your motives. Are you being sincere in your actions? Or are you just asking questions without caring about the answers?

Sincerity in action, words, and motivations will bring you satisfaction and help you maintain a reputable character as you continue to produce and build your way to your ultimate goal. People can detect insincerity and will turn away from it. Positive thoughts can also arise through sincere motivations and conversations even if you were feeling low to begin with.

WHERE TO GO FROM HERE

Increasing production levels as well as capability comes with experience, with reps, with collaboration and awareness. If you're doing something multifaceted, take advantage of your strong area of production and get help from others on your weak points. When you work with others, you will undoubtedly have some negative experiences as well as some positive results. Either way, you'll meet other individuals who can help you become more productive and you will help them be more productive as well.

When you are doing more work of this kind, collaborating or outsourcing, whatever you want to call it, you are by extension giving the others work to produce and a reason for doing so; and with the right connections, everyone's productivity increases. This is part of the magic.

Start with the right mindset.

Start with getting the mindset right. If you are in a place right now where you are looking for ideas on how to get more done, finish more, and keep up the motivation to do so, it starts in the mind. Start with a sense of awareness that everything is what it is and you are okay right now. Let go of that urgent-need-want-lack mindset. Patience and present-mindedness will be more useful right now.

Make sure you are competent at what you want to do. Make sure you are self-aware enough to know what you are good at and not just romanticizing an ideal that you wouldn't enjoy the work or training or education required to get you there.

Visualize your goal. Set your goals within that goal, the steps that will get you there. If you don't know them all at this point, that's fine. You know what the first step is and that is to start, more will be revealed to you from there. Live your goals, serve your goals, every action and reaction will be driven by and have at its root your goals.

Next, to do more, you have to desire to do more. And the reverse is true. The more you do the more you'll want to do. Sink into this process and embrace it and settle in for life. This is the key—when you want to be in the process more than you want the fruit of that process, that's when you've won.

SHARE YOUR KNOWLEDGE WITH OTHERS

You have likely achieved what you have achieved due in part to others' contributions, advice, writing, or speaking, etc. Now it's your turn to share with others who are trying to do what you do. Even if you don't know of anyone specifically who wants to learn from you, put your material out there, tell people what you've learned. It is amazing how frequently we use YouTube to fix something around the house, cook a new recipe, or find a blog that explains a particular problem that we could not otherwise solve.

The internet is filled with information, and it is uploaded by people who want to share with the world. Has it been helpful to you? If so, the way to show appreciation is also to offer what you have to others. It doesn't have to be in a public way like YouTube or other social media platforms, but think of ways to share what you've discovered so it can be available to help others.

How can you share your journey to higher production with others? Through what mediums can you make available what you have learned?

THE FINAL CHAPTER

When you realize that production is a state of mind, when you understand that your life is a story that you write, a story that you tell through whatever medium you choose, then you have begun to become the most productive version of yourself. Realizing the capacity of the mind to be one-tracked, you can figure out how to get into that zone of thinking that is in keeping with your ultimate goal.

The zone will become recognizable. It won't always be easy to channel it—oftentimes the key will be to learn how to let go of trying so that the thoughts can realign and you can start to absorb and observe patterns again, instead of forcing your own preconceived ideas upon freely rising thoughts. Let it be the other way. Consider each thought that arises and calmly notice the ones that are in alignment with your ultimate goal. Take these thoughts and let them form ideas and then go to work.

Take time for mental reboots.

This is why meditating and emptying your mind can be so useful. It's like a mental reboot. It's a clearing of space so new ideas can arise. For some, the benefits of meditation can be the same as the benefits they receive from working long hours and staying mentally in the work. I think this is rare in our society, however. If you're not a natural-born workaholic, try meditation.

Being at your productive best is not necessarily measurable by an outsider although of course they will weigh in with opinions. Your productive best is measured by *you.* By the way you feel when you go to sleep at night. By the progress you make toward your ultimate goal. Productivity at the highest levels is a lifestyle—just like the fitness experts, diet experts, investors, etc. They didn't get to where they are overnight or by doing one specific thing. It's a way of living.

Don't give up after a bad day. And don't give in just because of a bad day, telling yourself you'll try again tomorrow. Try again today.

But if you do go to bed completely disappointed in your day, in your lack of productivity, don't dwell on it. Tomorrow will be better. Say to yourself before you go to sleep, *Tomorrow will be better.* When you wake up in the morning, say, *Today's going to be a good day!* And then you don't have to wait any longer to make it so. You start doing.

As the hours pass by, you get work done and you enjoy the feeling of doing and completing it.

Some days there will be work around the house instead of work you can directly correlate with your ultimate goal. But remember, your family, the house, the external world you live in can affect your production and progress toward your ultimate goal as well. If things are broken at home, it weakens your productivity mindset when it comes to working toward your goal. Everything is connected.

There are some things you can cut out of your life, but your family and your home base are your sources of strength. Keep them well. It's all part of the productive state of mind.

ACKNOWLEDGMENTS

Thanks to...

Heather for the feedback and support, Dave Wildasin for the editorial direction, Eileen Rockwell for the awesome cover design, Terry Clifton for the excellent interior design, and Angela Shears for the valuable editing work.

ABOUT THE AUTHOR

JOHN MARTIN enjoys writing, reading, and studying personal development and human psychology. He is the author of *Empower Yourself,* a book about finding and achieving your personal vision of success.